THE
7 Slates
OF
Success

Wilson A. LaFaurie, Esq.

The 7 Slates of Success
Wilson A. LaFaurie

This book is based on true stories woven into
fictional characters.

Scripture verses are from the King James Version, KJV,
public domain.

ISBN#: 978-1-7327349-0-6 Softcover
ISBN#: 978-1-7327349-1-3 Kindle
ISBN#: 978-1-7327349-2-0 Epub

Editor: Joni Wilson
Cover design and interior design:
Deborah Perdue, Illumination Graphics
Cover artwork courtesy of Shutterstock
and Tara Thelen

Dedication

To my wife, Sharon N. LaFaurie, the F train,
and the book she was reading
the day we met.

Contents

Introduction

I have studied enough; I have succeeded enough; I have experienced enough; and I have lived and loved enough to write this story for you. Author Ernest Hemingway said, "In order to write about life first you must live it." We don't personally need to know one another for me to understand that we are connected on many levels, given that we are of the same species.

The genes of humans deviate oh so slightly. We have the same two sets of 23 chromosomes. Those are the chromosomes that distinguish us from animals, mammals, and all other creations. Those chromosomes, coupled with our genes, are basically organized in the exact same order, which I would argue means that our similarities are much greater than our distinctions. We share 99.5 percent of the same DNA.

There is no doubt in my mind that we are all brothers and sisters with our original mother born on a faraway continent. I hope that as you read this book and turn the pages you will bond with the characters, as if you knew them personally. Maybe you have encountered one of them in your life; we sometimes refer to them as angels. Some of us believe in only the things we can touch, smell, taste, see, and hear and others accept realms beyond that reality.

Evolution has dictated that humans have become more and more distant from one another. It seems to the naked eye that we are becoming less compassionate due to this separation. Most of today's human interactions are often via a computer or a phone screen. It is due to the technology era, which started in 1990, with the invention of the internet. *Always remember, every great gain travels with it a great loss.*

There was a time in society where humans interacted quite often in their trades, their churches, their stores, their neighborhoods, their organizations, and other community facets. Consider that many of today's relationships and marriages are commenced online, that our friends are now people we have never met, and that we buy our products by images on our computers from companies we have never walked inside of. The concept of person-to-person transactions are a thing of the past.

Take retail. Over the past ten years, there has been a retail apocalypse, malls having empty spaces, less traffic, and fewer employees. It is so common in North America that someone actually coined a phrase for it: "dead mall." This modern society has separated the interpersonal relationships between the employees and the customers. If we allow it, it is predicable that in the near future, elementary schools, junior high school, and high schools will be abolished with the same rationale that was used for converting past institutions. Look for the "dead school" coming soon to your nearby neighborhood.

Yes, I am ringing the warning bells on this one, because schools are the last vestige in society for children to develop emotionally and socially. Poor psychologist Sigmund Freud, the master of analyzing intricate bonds of relationships among humans. How would he view todays interpretation of "friends"?

As society keeps growing apart and human contact decreases, I hope that the lessons in this book find a way to mentor, teach, encourage, and motivate those individuals who wish to become successful, despite the cultural changes that have occurred. It has been said that "necessity is the mother of invention," so we now have what is called a life coach. These are dedicated professionals who have been certified to work with individuals to help them reach their goals, to work through their journeys and their dilemmas in life.

These trained experts mostly use proven techniques of problem solving by identifying them from the participants' feedback. Eventually, the recipient learns the techniques needed to apply in life, without the assistance of a life coach. Think about the time you rode your first bicycle and there were these training wheels on the left and the right of your back wheel, or when you took your first swim and you had the assistance of a floating device.

Life coaches are necessary in building *you*, when you are initially commencing or entering a new venue where there are many pitfalls that can negatively affect you in the long term. Life coaches exist in the corporate world, schools, hospitals, gyms, sports teams, and wherever there is a need. For those who want to commence their journey without a life coach, this book has meticulously developed principles that have been utilized by the most successful people in the world, whether the successful are aware that they are applying these principles is of consequence.

Remember, it was Socrates who asked the famous artist how he knew that his painting would become so popular. And it was the artist who had no substantive response. In other words, the artist who created the painting didn't realize what made the painting compelling to the human eye. Often, greatness just happens, due to certain principles being applied, yet the gifted believes that it was intention. It is only when someone like Socrates asked the right questions that they are exposed. So, I say to "the gifted," be humble or one day you might be exposed for unknowingly applying the laws of success.

As I have told many of my protégés in the past, scientist Sir Isaac Newton's law of universal gravitational is in action, whether you understand gravity or not. The same theory applies to the slates of success. It is by the past failures and the ultimate successes that these beliefs have been created. Learning, developing, and evolving in life require all of the resources one can get their hands on. Use the ideas in this book until the principles are ingrained into your way of thinking. Like all things that are practiced enough, they will ultimately become part of your muscle memory.

Still, to succeed there has never been or never will be a short path to fulfilling your life's goals. Do not be intimidated by commitment to yourself and to your goals. Do not fear success or failure. The struggle is rejuvenating, if you are not challenged, then you will find life stale. Many people find a safe profession and, in the end, they discover dissatisfaction. Seek the battle and the confrontation. Losing the confrontation doesn't change the idea that you can always go back to your fallback position; it means that you wish to test your capacities, test your potential.

The advantage that this writing renders to you is that it is an instruction manual on the mindset and the concepts necessary to attain your goals. The days of old and the challenges that existed in the times of the great writer Horatio Alger also exist today, but they are exponentially more arduous. Today, there are many more pitfalls to accomplishing your dreams. Consider the opioid epidemic, gang violence, broken family structures, and the issues of bullying in schools. The challenges for today's youth were not envisioned or anticipated by our predecessors. Young people, harken to this call, your reality is that you will need to be greater than the greatest of the past.

Does a person have to live a lifetime before being introduced to the correct belief system? I have never understood why society has accepted the concept of the school of hard knocks, as if success has to be learned through making the exact same mistakes that your predecessors made. Over the centuries, great men and women have succeeded, despite the era or the continent where they lived, or despite the particular micro-challenges of the times. Activist Martin Luther King Jr. confronted different obstacles than Steve Jobs, however, both men utilized the same principles to reach their mountaintop. So can you. This book, the life I have lived, and the teachers that I have had are now for your benefit and survival. Yes, survival is the word I chose.

This book is based on true stories woven into fictional characters. Do not let your guard down on what is reality and what is fairy tale, because in life the two can become one. I once observed a cat aggressively protecting an infant from an attacking dog, when the parents were not present. I mean the cat blocked the charging canine and chased it away from the danger zone. Do not limit the way you think, based on your past life experiences; fantasy and reality often coincide. My favorite storyteller,

Hans Christian Andersen, once stated, "Life itself is the most wonderful fairy tale."

So be aware, I also pose questions at the end of each chapter. The reason I use this method is because for over 25 years, I was trained as a trial lawyer, and I have always had success in getting to the right answers by posing the right questions. Imagine that you and I are in the same room. I would be able to cross-examine you, analyze your responses, and continue with a series of follow-up questions. When you answer the questions, imagine that you are on the witness stand.

Thank you for reading this book. Thank you for taking as many hours as it took to complete it, be it one, three, five, or more hours. My job has been completed if at the end of the book you can't decipher between the parts that are fiction and those that are nonfiction.

My thanks goes out to Brad Larochelle for coaching me in July 1983, when I was a junior in life. He died a few years back. Thank you to my grandmother, Casta Villarreal, for loving me unconditionally. Thank you to my daughter, Tabitha, for having that sparkle of life in her eyes. Thank you to my mother, Teresa, for willing to fight this cruel world all on her own. Thank you to my father, Antonio, for showing me what a gentleman looks like. Thank you to my daughter, Jessica, for following in my footsteps. Thank you to my brother, Jairo, for showing me what fearlessness looks like. Thank you to my sister, Francia, for showing me what peace looks like. Thank you to my earthly brother, Danny Brennan, for showing me what commitment looks like. I thank my wife, Sharon N. LaFaurie, for loving me in a greater way than Juliet loved Romeo and for being the most beautiful woman I have ever encountered.

Chapter 1

Success is stumbling from failure to failure
with no loss of enthusiasm.
—Winston Churchill

Over two-and-a-half decades have passed since I started my business, and I feel that I didn't store enough memories. I should have created a friendship book, a career book, a family book, and a life book with photos, documents, recordings, and anything that would have allowed me to have better recall later in years. One would think that with the twenty-five-year career I had as a criminal trial lawyer, I would remember more than I do. When I consider just the facets of my practice, I have represented over 4,000 individuals charged with crimes, stemming from a poor mother not having enough food in her refrigerator to a gang member shooting a rival, point blank in the head, with a .44 Magnum.

The genius of the brain is that it utilizes what is necessary and discards the trivial, especially over a challenged life span. I would love to remember the trivial! I can recall when I was accepted into law school and when I passed the New York bar exam, but I can't remember my financial struggles during that time and yet I was living in poverty. In my law practice, my brain was always being fed so much factual information on every case. Having folders filled with crime-scenes photos, witnesses testimony, charts, medical reports, videos, and audios could be overwhelming at times.

This is when autopilot kicks in, and the brain deciphers the relevant stuff from the superfluous material. Imagine this process going on over a twenty-five-year period with thousands of case folders. It makes common sense that details are no longer in detail form, they are less than a faint memory! Whenever I am moving to a different office, rearranging new furniture, or just doing spring cleaning is when I discover items from my past cases that are incredibly enlightening! Particularly letters from past clients. Rarely do I remember the person who wrote it, how they appeared, or the sound of their voice, however, to them I am ingrained in their cerebrum. And inmates are never shy to express themselves.

These are the two most recent letters that I stumbled onto.

October 26, 2013
Green Haven Correctional Facility
594 Route 216
Stormville, New York 12582

Dear Walter,

I hope this letter finds you in God's blessings.
As for me, I just wanted to reach out to you to
tell you that I appreciate what you did for me.
My end date where they can hold me is soon
approaching: December 1, 2014. I don't know
what I will do with my life after they release
me, but I do know that if I didn't have you as my
lawyer I would never see my child, Tamasha, or
my mother. I have never been a religious person
but I know that you were given to me by God.
There are so many brothers here that are facing
trial, and they will serve the rest of their lives
behind these brick walls. I tell all of them about
you, but they have nobody to pay you.

There is a guy named Korey Lochsmith who
has been in here for over twelve years and everyone in prison knows that he is innocent. He was
convicted after a Queens jury convicted him, with
no DNA, no video, no confession, and no credible
eyewitnesses. Everyone knows Queens juries

are fucked up. I know you're a good man and a great lawyer. I ask you to take a look at his case and you will see that they are killing an innocent man. Sorry to ramble about this hellhole, and I must leave know for chow. God bless you and your family and your daughters.

Sincerely and forever grateful,
Jean O'Reilly
B&C# 4522540M

Here is the second one from a client . . . a friend.

Dear Mr. Walter L.,

My blessings to you, your family, career, and life. I thank you again for your hard work and all your time that you worked with me. I hope all is well with you. I know it's been some time. But I will NEVER forget you. I pray for you every day and thank God that I met you!

I have been trying to adjust, the state is a little different than the city. I was in reception for two months at my final spot. I have a vocation as a carpenter. I now work as a porter in the afternoon. I was also working at Ulster. I am on a baseball team and staying out of trouble; the hard part is so being alone. I haven't spoking to anyone in five months, no one visits, it's hard to write cause of money (surcharges) issues.

I do not know if anyone knows where I am at all, but I am ok now. I just found out I can send letters as "legal mail," so I just want you to know I love you and never will forget you. I don't like the way the judge was. He said he was gonna be fair, but he always stopped you from showing our proof. Didn't he see that if I didn't fight back against Darrell, I would have died? My mother is sick, and she doesn't come to Ulster, she's still mad 'cause of the rent that she can't pay. I feel like I let everyone down. I tell everyone in here about you like you are Johnny C. I will forever think about what you did for me.

Beloved,
K. Thomas

Every seven years, I would shred case files that were in my storage, and I would be reminded of the thousands of people who I had assisted in these ordeals. At other times, I would be shopping in the mall with my wife, walking through the busy streets in Brooklyn, or watching a junior league soccer game and someone would recognize me with a, "Sir, if it wasn't for you, my life would have been destroyed . . . in the ruins." I did not dare ask, for the sake of embarrassing him in public how I helped.

I do recall once browsing through a local pharmacy store and a young employee in his early thirties staring in my direction. "Are you Walter?" Not recognizing why he was asking, but answering in the affirmative, he commenced to put his work tablet on the shelf and extended his hand in my direction. As I shook his hand, he drew me closer and hugged me.

"You, my man, believed in me when everyone else convicted me just on her word!"

Being humble, I responded with, "Bro . . . it was the DNA science that cleared you and . . . "

Without being able to finish my sentence, he started laughing out loud and in his native Brooklyn accent stated, "You buggin u da best!"

I smiled and responded, "I am so glad we won that one!"

I always walk away feeling unfulfilled, knowing that there are thousands of other innocent lives who will not be spared, will not have the same fate. I think to myself, *Saving one person at a time just doesn't cut it.*

These encounters remind me of why I walked away from the courtroom. Didn't I realize as an adult that fairness and justice are nor equally spread? As a child, we believe that Santa Claus delivers gifts to all children . . . right? As an adult, why was I so offended by an erroneous verdict? I finally figured out that when the jury convicted one of my innocent clients, three things occurred, three emotions came to light. One, an innocent person would be behind metal bars, brick walls, and be treated like cattle. Two, all the midnight candles I burned preparing for this case had been for naught. Three, the jury personally rejected me, and I was inadequate in explaining to them his innocence!

Welcome to the *land of inequities*. Within these life's inequities, the dawning of revelations some-times occur, Miguel de Cervantes was incarcerated in the Crown Jail of Seville twice from the years of 1597 to 1602. While in prison, he drafted the first novel in modern literature history, *The Ingenious Nobleman Sir Quixote of La Mancha*, better known as *Don Quixote*.

There were memorable moments and accom-plishments in my long career, including acquittals on jury trials that left judges befuddled and angry. Yes, the neutral and objective judge was partisan. As a human, I had cases that I didn't personally want to win, my client was the definition of guilty, however, my profession has called for all lawyers to represent clients "zealously" without question! Whether a person is innocent or guilty is of no consequence. I have taken an oath in the federal and state courts to protect every American who is forced to sit in the defendant's chair.

Somehow, 223 years ago, the US Constitution was signed by twelve state delegates, protecting the rights of the citizens, yet the average citizen still does not embrace it. Oh, if I had a dime for every person who asked me, "How could you represent a guilty person?" Without hesitation, I would always rebut them with a question, never an answer, "How could a law enforcement agent arrest an innocent person, and how could a judge allow that conviction?" Afterwards, there was always silence, never a response from these accusers. It is my belief that the mob mentality will always be a knee-jerk reaction to anyone who has been accused of a crime. Maybe the concept of an eye for an eye is ingrained in human nature. Naturalist Charles Darwin was correct when he stated that the evolution of humans and the shedding of our inner primates takes successive generations.

During the heyday of my criminal practice, I can still recall how I dismantled so many so-called famous people during cross-examination. Not to mention the other conniving witnesses who had an axe to grind against my client. Days leading up to any trial, every morning at 8:45 a.m., I recall walking through the fourth floor of the criminal court building, this is where all of the police officers waited to be called as witnesses in the "people's direct case-in-chief." As I walked pasted thirty or more officers, I pretended that I had not noticed them. They, on the other hand, made it clear that they knew who I was, not in a bad way but in a high school manner, you know like when students murmur behind the teacher's back. As often stated, "safety in numbers." On their defense, I attributed it to anxiety, nothing malicious.

There was something genuine about honest police officers that I admired. Even the ones who did not experience my cross-examinations in the past twenty years still understood who I was, the suntanned man in a light-gray, flannel, pinstripe suit walking and talking like a surgeon before the scalpel is drawn. I was the guy who was going to bring discomfort to their lives for the next four hours. Worse yet! They knew that the jury was probably going to acquit my client of all charges.

After every acquittal, I had to stand before the local news channels and explain why it was not a runaway jury. Funny how they never asked me that question when my client was convicted. I have seen hundreds of people celebrate the conviction of an innocent man. I have also witnessed the same defendant be proclaimed innocent after that verdict was overturned based on forensics and the confession of the real perpetrator.

I believe embedded in all of us is the trait of vengeance, and it is also the culprit of all erroneous convictions. Our criminal justice system has one monumental flaw, that is, that jurors have inherit bias against a person called a defendant. Have you ever heard how a judge instructs every juror on day one, "Members of the jury, today you will hearing a case that is titled, The People of the State of New York v. Mark Denn." That pronouncement is already telling the jurors that the good community is against the defendant. It is at that moment that most innocent defendants realize that the system is stacked against them.

I chose this career roughly twenty-five years ago, and it all seems but a blur! I do not remember all of the details of all of my failures, however, every so often they do pop up in an attempt to remind me of my weaknesses.

As an adolescent, I was confident, until failure introduced itself to me, then I would second-guess myself and create another game plan. But the vicious cycle of failure would repeat itself, because it is known that failure is always a nearby neighbor. There is an old verse that goes something like this. "If a person begins life with confidence, that person will end life in doubt, however, if that person begins life with doubt, that person will end life in confidence." Wow, did I learn the hard way that confidence, ambition, grit, motivation, tenacity, courage, drive, and discipline are *hollow until they are filled with content, otherwise, they are empty pleasantries, just nouns.*

Before I was given the tools to overcome the inequities of life, my life was laced with confusion, negativity, struggles, and failure. Over and over again, I would ask myself, "What is the point?" Were life's struggles just a lab experiment? If I had watched the movie *Hunger Games* as a teenager, I would have believed it was a documentary. It always seemed to me that I had to endure more than I was capable of enduring. Maybe I was weak, but God only knows; I always felt that the most difficult problems surfaced in my life and made their appearances at my most vulnerable times.

Somehow I made it past all the pitfalls and graduated from law school! I can still picture me, that young, Hispanic kid, sitting on the stoop of the house, on Ridgedale Avenue, waiting for the mail carrier to deliver the results of my bar exam. Without passing the bar exam, I wouldn't be certified to represent clients in the courtroom, and that was the only thing that the law meant to me. I envisioned myself standing in front of a judge and a jury, petitioning them to free an innocent man. As I'm daydreaming, I looked up and saw the mail carrier three feet away from me, with a hand extended toward me. I asked, "How did you know that I was waiting for my bar results?"

He looked at me and stated, "Kid, I wanted to be a lawyer when I was young, but my girlfriend became pregnant, and that's when my dream ended!" He continued, "I became aware two times a year when the results of the bar exam were released, and I started delivering early, because I knew that someone will fulfill their dreams. At forty years old, I know that what I do for a living is an honest living, and I guess it was for me!"

As I opened the white envelope, I saw on the top the letter: BAR RESULTS: PASS. As my eyes watered and I became emotional, Robert, the mail carrier, gave me a half-hearted hug, put his head down, and walked away. After that delivery of mail, I have never seen him again. I hope his career was the only thing he resigned! The next day a young, Hispanic woman, about the age of twenty-three delivered our mail. I did not have the courage to ask her why she joined the post office nor the courage to ask about Robert.

I can remember when I first launched my criminal practice with the hopes of being the next Clarence Darrow. Before the ink was dry on my law school certificate, I received a reality check from life. Nine months after putting up my shingle, my business was facing bankruptcy, as there were not enough clients. It would have been logical and pragmatic to concede defeat! My natural instinct was to take down the shingle with my name on it and apply to a law firm, which would have meant money, insurance, and stability.

However, it was time again to find which principle applied to this hopeless situation. I didn't want to be dumb about it, I just wished to keep my firm and my dream opened until all the possibilities had been exhausted. Then, somehow, by these laws of success, this belief system in my possession, my dream of running my own law practice lived on. I was able to bounce back before the final curtain, and it worked. Nothing particularly special happened, I just applied a principle to the issue that was defeating me. I was experiencing a second wind and a new life was inhaled into me.

Contrast that with when I was younger and full of confidence, anytime I would hit a wall or rejection, I would fold my tent, bury my tail, and quietly walk away. Because of the new principles I followed, I no longer relied on old beliefs, but what I have learned, what was taught to me by the gift I was given. I hate to complain, but I wish I'd had these principles when I was in junior high school. What a life changer that would have been. Was someone intentionally keeping them in a vault . . . shared only by a few?

Pierre, oh, Pierre, I can remember our daily chats. It is true that we never appreciate the greatness of a moment in life until it is long past us. What a cruel plight for humankind—the inability to live in the moment and constantly reminisce about a moment that has fleeted. It is rare in life to meet someone who proclaims, "These are the best moments of my life!" However, it is all too common to meet people who speak about a past glorious moment.

That old, angelic-looking man who would ride his bicycle down Middle Country Road in Centereach, New York. Anyone who has driven a car or ridden on a bicycle knew that Middle Country Road was a rattrap, buyer beware. It was everyone's assumptions that the road had so many potholes and orange cones on it because of uninterested, local politicians. According to Suffolk County accident statistics, that single road had more accidents in a six-month time period than any other road in the county.

Oddly enough, it never stopped that little old French man from peddling his old bike five miles per day from the grocery store to the church . . . twice a day. That old man seemed to have no family, no friends, and no home. His appearance would make one believe that he was illiterate, homeless, and lacked survival skills, however, given his physical strength, his daily endeavors, and his fearlessness, one could not conclude that he was one of the weak links in society. Therein lay the contradiction in the man named Pierre, his appearance stated one thing, but his actions spoke differently. If you told me that he had been on the earth for over 2,000 years, I would not take that as fantastical.

I met Pierre at the church; most people who attended the church were upper middle class or upper class, financially. Given all of the rich folks who attended the church regularly, no one ever questioned the obvious, that is, how did he survive in a suburban county, such as Suffolk, for so many years, at his age, without any family, real friends, or village support? Where did Pierre live? How is it that he was always smiling, always hugging people, and always giving advice to those who had ears?

Decades later, after meeting him, I do believe in the supernatural. That has been a long time ago, but I still envision my encounters with him, my walks, my talks, and my laughter with him. He left two gifts for me before he left me alone, here on earth. Gift number one is the gift of monetary success, and gift number two is the gift of happiness. The gift of worldly success, I now bestow on thee. The gift of happiness and spiritual success, I might never share with the world; I believe his intention was for me to share with the world the issues of monetary gains, not the spiritual gains. It is true that some things in one's life should be sheltered in one's heart.

Many people ask me about Pierre, including Nadira, my wife. They ask me if I think he is still alive. My answer is always the same. Death is not preordained; death is not on an egg timer or an hourglass, According to Genesis in the Bible,

Adam died at the age of 930 years. And, not to be outdone, Methuselah, the son of Enoch, lived until the age of 969. Poor Enoch wasn't as healthy as his son; he passed at the young age at 365. Yes, Pierre can still be alive!

Chapter 2

Believers, look up—take courage.
The angels are nearer than you think.

—Billy Graham

In my childhood, I was raised going to Catholic school, and somehow throughout my life, I have always found myself fascinated by all aspects of churches, the structure itself. All denominations pique my interest. I did "church crashing" for over a decade—that's where you go to a different church every Sunday, shake everyone's hand, and never return to that church again. My guess is that I never wanted to get tied down to any one way of thinking.

I invented my own hobby, it's called a "church collector," a person who photographs and captures images of all parts of churches, such as the pews, the podium, the cross on the top like a Christmas tree star, the sign outside with a weekly scripture, and the sculptures within. I have a binder with 407 photos of churches of various denominations, throughout continents, countries, and states.

Why is this any different than being a bird watcher? I have traveled to capture images of Cathedral de Santa Catalina in Cartagena, Colombia; St Peter's Basilica in Rome, Italy; Saint Basil's Cathedral in Moscow, Russia; Notre-Dame in Paris, France; Crystal Cathedral in Garden Grove, California, and Church of the Nativity in Bethlehem. Walking down the brick roads in Cartagena, encountering all the vendors, peddlers, and homeless on the street, I was reminded of the desperation depicted in many Winslow Homer landscape paintings.

However, when I approached the famous Santa Catalina Catholic church, I was instantly reminded of a beacon of light, a magnificent image. As prodigious as the most famous churches are around the world, the ones I adore are the cozy, little ones in unknown rural communities. Yes, it is awe-inspiring to walk into St. Peter's Basilica in Rome; it is overwhelming to stand inside it. You can feel the spirit of St. Peter, the right-hand disciple of Jesus in the building. The fact that his tomb is inside the church is mind blowing.

But the tiny, local churches, you know the ones where you have cross over a duck pond and a mile of dirt road to reach them. My guess is that God spends way more time in poor churches than he does in the wealthy churches.

> *And it came to pass, that, as Jesus sat*
> *at meat in his house, many publicans*
> *and sinners sat also together with*
> *Jesus and his disciples: for there were*
> *many, and they followed him.*
> *And when the scribes and Pharisees*
> *saw him eat with publicans and*
> *sinners, they said unto his disciples.*
> *How is it that he eateth and drinketh*
> *with publicans*
> *and sinners?*
> *When Jesus heard it, he saith unto*
> *them, They that are whole have no*
> *need of the physician, but they that*
> *are sick: I came not to call the righ-*
> *teous, but sinners*
> *to repentance.*
> —Mark 2:15–17, KJV

My fascination for these buildings eventually paid off. I think I was looking for a permanent church to attend and all the browsing and poking that I was doing with church watching would be similar to the person going out on a lot of dates. One early, Sunday morning, as I had finished moving into my new apartment near Lake Ronkonkoma, New York, I decide to peruse the neighborhood. A little closer to the water and right next to the baseball field, I spotted, yes, another church. Running out of time, having to build my furniture, and set up my new rig, I headed back home and made a mental note to myself about the find.

About three weeks later, on another Sunday morning, I drove back to the baseball field location wearing my best dating outfit. As I drove into the parking lot, I noticed over twenty men directing the traffic into this house of God. It reminded me of the one and only time I drove to North Carolina to see a NASCAR event. It was laborious driving from Long Island to Concord, and, once we arrived, we had to park in a dirt lot about 500 feet from the stadium.

It was the walk on this dirt road heading for this spectacular event that summoned my sensations. I don't know how to explain it, but some walks in life that lead to a particular destination can never be forgotten. Some lead to a beautiful place and others lead to a dreadful one! I think someone should write a book about famous "walks" in the context of history. Some immediately stand out, like the walk that Moses took when the Red Sea parted, or the walk that Martin Luther King Jr. took on his march for civil rights, or the road to Calvary, or the walk that millions of unknown immigrants make to find a promised land.

One of the differences at the NASCAR event was that people were so pissed about the parking disorganization, they freely expressed themselves through their vulgarity and loudness. But not here at the Jubilation Road church, where everyone was smiling, as if they weren't pissed-off deep down inside. In retrospect, it was a riot to see people smile and say, "Praise God, brother!" when you know they really wished to say, "This is bullshit . . . out of my way!"

As I walked into this church, there must have been over 1,000 people in the congregation. As we all selected our own seats, I saw this unkempt, undiagnosed, crazy-looking man staring at me, and he was walking directly with laser focus in my direction. Jesus, first day at this church and I had become the target of this Wile E. Coyote-looking guy. Lucky me, I thought, *Should I just turn my back and act as if I didn't see him, give him the shoulder?*

What's weird was that the surrounding people at the church were moving out of his way, as if he were parting the Red Sea. How in a shitstorm did he know that I was the new recruit? I was no more than forty feet inside this building. Maybe Grandma Casta was correct when she told me that some people have the "sinner's face." If I had the "sinner's face," how would I camouflage it?

So I broke into this full-blown grin, like I belonged, like the holy spirit was dancing in my pants. That didn't fool him! *Ok*, I thought, *can I give this old guy the shoulder?* Nah, everyone was now watching this unannounced meet and greet! But why did it look like he had no brakes on his feet, like he was gonna tackle me? I am six foot one, 190; he was five foot five and couldn't weigh more than a jockey . . . max of 130. He put his arms up, like he was coming in for a landing, and embraced me as if he were my father and I was the prodigal son returning from a life of sin and debauchery.

With a cat-eating smile, he yelped his name. "Pierre! Pierre Smith! Jesus *loves* you! He loves you . . . he loves you, brother!" I interpreted that as "Here's a sinner, sinner over here, sinner!" Then he proceeded to hold my hand in front of 1,000 strangers. Let me repeat that, he actually held my hand!

Oh, God, this was going from bad to worst. I think, *Now I appreciate the magic in "safe spaces."* Here, when I thought it couldn't get any more uncomfortable, the church members began to sing out loud, and this Pierre guy started speaking in tongues. I didn't know there was such a thing . . . wish I was prepared for this religious chanting. Had I walk into a satanic gathering? How far were the exits?

I turned my head gingerly toward the doors, not to draw more attention. I saw four burly men by the exit doors, with their arms crossed looking directly at me. This seemed really well-planned, maybe it's a mob thing. Luckily, for me, I was able to unhinge Pierre's hand at the twenty-minute mark, because he would suddenly catnap anytime the preacher paused to pour himself a drink of water. It all ended without any human sacrifices, and I walked so fast out of there that my hips were swinging a full east-west direction. If I never went back to that church, it would be too soon. Although I still have a photo of the outside.

Over and over, I would see that old man, not at the Jubilation Road church, but at a grocery store, riding his bike in the middle of traffic, and walking in the rain with no umbrella. Maybe I had always passed him but never noticed him. Have you ever had that happen to you, where you meet someone and then you're bumping into them at every turn and corner? Truthfully, I never gave it any further thought.

One day I was grocery shopping at Waldbaums supermarket, and by the pastry section, I saw that old man. With a white, long-sleeve shirt, looking disheveled, he was sitting where they had samples of crumb cake for customers to taste. I got out of range so he wouldn't see me, as I didn't want a repeat of our first encounter. I also noticed that he had eaten the entire pie, sample by sample, until the pie tin was empty. Then he walked over to the dairy section and poured himself three cups of milk, I am talking about those big red Solo cups, famous at football and tailgating parties.

I could not leave him, knowing what I just saw. So my heart got the best of me. I walked up to him and when he saw me his eyes went high beam! Oh, oh! what had I done? But he never charged, he walked toward me with a slight limp, and his face full of white crumb cake powder. I asked him if he would have dinner with me. He accepted and the rest is history.

He spent the next seven months living with me. He had no home, no family, no identification, and no pedigree information. I once asked him his age, and his response was "A little younger than President Ronald Reagan." What month was the president born, I asked. He replied, "Not really sure." Then he would rhythmically rub his head, as if he kept rubbing the answer would magically appear in his brain. He would ultimately walk away with a beet-red forehead, and I would walk away not knowing his pedigree.

Not sure why, but I have always stayed rather quiet when I am with the elderly. I believe it a sign of respect and a way for me to listen twice as much as I speak. With Pierre, it was no different, even though he wasn't a scholar, a poet, a philosopher, or a teacher. I still waited for his words, his reactions, and mostly his contagious grin, as it would come out of nowhere—it even surprised him. He would follow it up with laughter. "What is so funny?' I once asked. A straight answer was never forthcoming with that old, childish man. Although I must say that there was something so inconsistent about his personality, not in a horribly bad way but in an intriguing manner.

Every morning when I would get up, Pierre would not be at the house and there was always a note left for me. His words were well-groomed, and they had an uncanny way of addressing my concerns for the day. Maybe he was listening to me twice as much as I was to him? On this particular Friday, I found this note.

> *You have found your home, and it is not made of material; it is made of people.*

He left me 206 life notes within that time period. I saved each one as if they were the Dead Sea Scrolls. I hope one day to share them with the world! As he was living with me, I never felt that he was a stranger or an outsider, on the other hand, it felt like he was my grandpa. None of his daily habits seemed strange, nor did I have to change any of my everyday tasks. Often people would ask me with an uncomfortable look, "Hey, how's Pierre, is he still living with you?" After many months of having him stay with me, I realized people saw me as strange. It was relayed to me that I wasn't getting invited to "house worship nights" where a group of men would talk about family, struggles, and likes, because they knew I would bring "Sancho Panza."

I once took Pierre to Jamaica, Queens, where Grandma Casta lived. At age eighty, she still had the greatest sense of honor that I have ever known.

My visits to Casta's apartment were as random as the lottery, without any notice, but she somehow always knew when I would appear, because she had the Colombian food ready for me. Casta had lived in the same apartment since 1973; there were six apartment buildings with four floors each. Everyone in that low-income neighborhood knew who she was, the little coffee-colored Colombian woman who fed all the homeless adults and babysat all the low-income neighborhood children in those buildings. I recall once going to visit her and running into Packo, when he was leaving his two little girls with Casta. She raised him when he was a child and now, two decades later, she was doing the same for his kids . . . imagine that. She did this for four decades. Anytime I would visit Casta in her one-bedroom apartment, there was always someone eating a meal that she had cooked for them.

On this particular day, I entered her apartment, 2D, with Pierre. She first looked at him and he then looked at her. One would think that they had met before. Then she looked at me and gave me the biggest grin that I had ever seen her release. Casta was always happy, but she would rarely have a grin on her face. Often I would take her shopping or to a Colombian festival, and anytime she would see somebody who had too big of a smile on their face, she would impulsively say something sarcastic in Spanish like, "Who's tickling her butt?" or "If he keeps that mouth open, he's gonna catch plenty of those overweight flies."

On the day that I took Pierre to her apartment, in her native language, she asked me, "le hago un plato de comida, a el christiano tambien?" (Should I make him, the Christian, a plate of food?) I responded, "Abuela, miralo, que tu piensas?" (Grandma, look at him, what do you think?) Casta started walking toward the kitchen. "Ok, mi estas diciendo que el come como un camello!" Yes, Grandma! Pierre eats like a camel. Pierre looked at Casta with a smile and rubbed his tummy like he was a Christian buddha. She continued to give him the shoulder, and he continued to rub his stomach until she served him arroz con pollo.

As I sat with them at the table, I looked at Pierre. He had not spoken a word as he was mechanically shoveling food in his mouth like he was a Class A crane operator. Then I looked at her, and she was just watching him eat. She looked over at me with her spunky wit and stated, "Tell him that he almost ate the fork." I laughed. Pierre raised his head for a second and gave out a belly laugh, as if he knew what she had just stated, then he went right back to the bowl.

To say the least, it was an interesting encounter to witness the two greatest people who I had ever known come together. I have always imagined in my mind the encounter between Jesus of Nazareth and John the Baptist or the encounter between Socrates and Aristotle. And here I was, introducing Casta to Pierre, wow, a moment that I would forever cherish.

As we left Casta's apartment, I gave her the biggest hug and slipped seventy dollars into her pocket. Her last words to me were "cuidate antiguo!" Translation, "Take care, ancient." I was twenty-six at the time; she was eighty.

Five months passed, and Pierre and I were celebrating Thanksgiving together. Pierre said he had a gift for me, but it was too heavy for him to carry into the house. As we went outside, I noticed an old, large box on the back of his bicycle. It was sitting on what looked like a homemade, do-it-yourself, wood crate. I didn't know what to make of it and kept staring at it without knowing what was in the crate. I turned to Pierre to thank him but he was already inside the house.

I was able to get the box into the house, and there I noticed Pierre chomping on the Entenmann's butter cake. Pierre was grinning from ear to ear as I entered the house with the box. "Jesus is good! Are you so happy . . . are you so happy now, brother?" he bellowed at me. At the moment I had no idea what he was referring to. Then instantly, he became serious and instructed me not to open the box until I felt ready to learn the rules of "worldly success." Then, with his childish grin, without any questions from me, he stated, "But it's not as good as heavenly success!"

It was the first time that I heard his voice inflection change to suit his age, it made me want to open the box, but it made me want to know more about the second box even more. Then, before I was able to ask him more about this "heavenly success," he shouted out, "Turkey time . . . brother, it's turkey time!" I paused and looked at him, puzzled, thinking, *How does this cake monster know anything about food preparation?*

"Pierre, I am the cook! Soon enough the meal will be ready." Then, at that exact moment, the oven timer interrupted me with the ringer, over and over again.

"Brother, it's turkey time" he said with that twinkle. "That turkey has good butter on it!" Then, for the first time since I'd met him, I noticed his eyes. They reminded me of the sky-blue marbles I played with when I was a child, and it dawned on me that he was rocking some beautiful, white hair.

Yes, I loved Pierre, including his musty, old, smelly, old-man, white shirts.

After Thanksgiving, I never saw him again . . . I think.

Chapter 3

*In Hinduism, Shiva is a deity who represents transformation. Through destruction and restoration, Shiva reminds us that **endings are beginnings**, and that our world is constantly undergoing a **cycle of birth, death and rebirth.***
—Karen Salmansohn, bold emphasis added

I woke up and Pierre wasn't present. I looked out my window, and his light-blue, rusty bike was also gone, the bike with the fruit basket clipped to the handlebars and wood planks on the back. I walked around the apartment to look for signs of his present or past . . . nothing! How could such an old man leave absolutely no signs of life? In the past, anytime I would turn my back on him or get distracted by another event, he would always disappear.

I never understood why he did that, was he multitasking relationships? This was the same guy who always had powdered sugar all over his lips, chin, and shirt. As I sat by myself, I started to second-guess his existence . . . until I noticed that brown box. As I walked to the front door, a note was left for me. It was message 206 that he had written for me, and sadly the last. It read as follows.

> *Everyone you will encounter is your friend;*
> *they just don't know it yet?*

On December 1, 1997, at 3:30 a.m., I woke up restless, unable to sit in bed, read a book, or watch an old movie on television. So I finally walked over to the box. I opened it, and all I saw were books. They were old books, some of the authors and titles were unknown to me, like the book on Taoism and the book on Zen. There was a spectrum of subjects and figures, such as Benjamin Franklin, Descartes, Aristotle, Plato, Kant, Hobbes, Saint Augustine, Locke, Hume, Carnegie, Allen, Peale, Emerson, and nineteen others. At the moment, I was interested, but disinterested, in these books.

I randomly picked one of them up, and I noticed on the inside cover there was the number twenty-four. I picked up another book, and it was labeled five, the next was labeled eleven. It appeared that someone had taken a lot of time and effort to put them in chronological order. My disinterest started to dissipate, and my interest began to grow. Also in that box there were hundreds of handwritten pages, front and back, hundreds of pages of science experiments, diagrams, and calculations from astronomy and theological interpretations. I also noticed that the box contained five Bibles: Ethiopian, Christian, Hebrew, Catholic, and Protestant. Only one of them had handwritten interpretations. That Bible had a total of seventy-three books within it. Now my curiosity was piqued, anything having to do with the church was my Achilles heel.

So at that moment, I decided that I would embark on this unknown journey. I recognized how challenging this would be. I committed to read each work in the order that was proposed to me by the attached note, not skipping a single page. Every morning, I would read for two hours; it was always pitch black out with a pure silence. Then when I returned home from work, I would read until I fell asleep, usually about midnight.

The first year, I followed this schedule faithfully. The next two years, I resigned my job and moved in with my mother, Teresa, where she had lived alone in Queens Village. Most of her life she had lived alone .

. . it's her strong sense of independence that was programmed into her as a child, when she was abandoned by her father. Every day there is a new Teresa being born in this world. I hope those children can succeed, despite their lack of family.

All I did during those two years was read, interpret, and write. My mother, being a busy executive, always prepped my meals on Sunday for the upcoming week. Compulsively, I took notes while I read, because I felt that the information was speaking directly to me. It was like I was hearing the author's voices as I read every word. Each new book spoke to me in a distinctively different voice and inflection, at times that was as fascinating as the subject matter that I was consuming. One would never think of Benjamin Franklin as a person who had more faults and weaknesses than the average person.

Here is Franklin's personal list of thirteen virtues as written in his autobiography.

- **Temperance**. Eat not to dullness; drink not to elevation.
- **Silence**. Speak not but what may benefit others or yourself; avoid trifling conversation.
- **Order**. Let all your things have their places; let each part of your business have its time.

- **Resolution.** Resolve to perform what you ought; perform without fail what you resolve.
- **Frugality.** Make no expense but to do good to others or yourself; i.e., waste nothing.
- **Industry.** Lose no time; be always employ'd in something useful; cut off all unnecessary actions.
- **Sincerity.** Use no hurtful deceit; think innocently and justly, and, if you speak, speak accordingly.
- **Justice.** Wrong none by doing injuries, or omitting the benefits that are your duty.
- **Moderation.** Avoid extremes; forbear resenting injuries so much as you think they deserve.
- **Cleanliness.** Tolerate no uncleanliness in body, cloaths, or habitation.
- **Tranquillity.** Be not disturbed at trifles, or at accidents common or unavoidable.
- **Chastity.** Rarely use venery but for health or offspring, never to dullness, weakness, or the injury of your own or another's peace or reputation.
- **Humility.** Imitate Jesus and Socrates.

Another interesting thing started to occur, as I was deeper into the book list. I started to realize the errors and flaws that certain great people made in their lives by the later books that I read. Meaning that the principles and precepts in book eight addressed the issues and problems of the characters in earlier books. In my imagination, I envisioned one book dressed as a human, giving worldly advice to another book. It became apparent to me that the chronological order of the books was based on a hierarchy of learning. I pictured Descartes doubting Saint Augustine, and Socrates cross-examining Thomas Hobbes. It's the battle of the ages that everyone should pay top billing to observe.

As I was doing all this work and edification, I miraculously didn't feel like I was being frivolous with my time. Yet, I had no game plan or any explanation as to why I spent 1,095 days in this laborious task. In reading all this material, I was operating in a realm of faith. My belief was based on a man named Pierre. I know that when he handed me the box with all the worldly knowledge, he would not have done so if it was not going to change the way people think about success and failure. I just knew in my heart of hearts that the material in that box contained the answers that would make the poor . . . rich! Often in life I have felt as if someone or something directed my path to safety or success, particularly during the most difficult times.

On the thirty-first day of July, I had completed all of my work on these books. I ended with thirty-four composition books, with 100 pages per book, the black-and-white books we used when we were younger. Each time I had finished another book, I felt that my way of thinking about worldly success had started to change. I also realized that the concepts of each book had started to merge. One would think that the authors of each book had conspired together with the other authors to proclaim these principles of worldly success.

When I reached the final book number, I felt that I had the cure to a fatal disease and that I had the calling to tell people about these interwoven beliefs. One day, I heard the distinct voice of a man that went from sinner to saint, that was the voice of Saint Augustine, "The truth is like a lion; you don't have to defend it. Let it loose; it will defend itself."

One late night, after much reading and writing, I fell asleep on my futon. The next morning, I remembered a dream that I had. I was walking past the Manhattan Detention Complex, better known as "The Tombs" to New Yorkers, when all of a sudden falling from the sky comes down hundreds of books. They landed adjacent and next to one another. But the books were not shaped rectangularly, they were shaped as individual puzzle pieces. And after hitting the concrete street, they all fit perfectly together, creating a portrait of a brown brick elementary school.

A jail and an elementary school in the same dream how ironic!

After I had finish the thirty-fourth book, I was convinced that I was sitting on an organized belief system that would take people out of their poverty. Through my interpretation of each book, I wrote down the key messages that the author intended to relay. Some books consisted of as little as three messages, and other books had well over fifty messages. At that juncture, I was holding thirty-four individual summaries, and I knew that I wanted to compare each book to see if there was any consistency. During this process, I used five full bottles of Visine on my dry eyes, but I still lost part of my vision during this construction.

In my mother's living room, I placed on the floor all of the letter-size, page summaries and started to make notes about any common themes. As I did this, I was eerily struck and reminded of my recent dream and the puzzle.

I had finally finished! I wished that I could go back to my normal life, but that was not reality. I felt like Peter after he met the Nazarene!

Depression set in, because it dawned on me that nobody would believe me if I told them that all of the most successful people in history have the exact system of success, even though they are separated by thousands of years. *This system on worldly success can be divided into seven rules.*

So a small part of my earlier dream was now transparent to me. That is, that I was given these books, and that they were really individual messages by some of the most successful people in history. However, the part of the dream that showed a jail and the school befuddled me for over twenty years.

But what should I do with my findings? Three years and one day of this endeavor for what application? I didn't know the answer to that particular question, so I would use this belief for selfish reasons, to become a private pilot, a motivation speaker, an author of books, and a trial lawyer, maybe a famous one.

Chapter 4

Education is what remains after one has forgotten what one has learned in school.

—Albert Einstein

I started asking myself some fundamental questions about my upbringing. Why didn't middle schools or high schools teach fundamental principles of success in all those years? How long should society wait until it teaches children or young adults how to set goals, organize and plan financially, leadership skills, investing, mentoring, and conquering low self-esteem? Aren't those skills equal to art, music, and physical education? When was the last time our leaders of academia looked at the modern problems associated with youth development and addressed them with classes in our schools?

It is time to rearrange the educational system from elementary school through high school. Charles Darwin was correct about the survival of the fittest, but does that mean that we as a society should just sit and watch the unfit drown? We have evolved since Darwin! We are way past an antiquated society that sits around watching the less fortunate fail. We as a society have a mandate to assist these children. We can educate and we can empower today's youth, early in life before the challenges overtake them.

The reason that the US has the strongest military in the world is because it has invested time and resources into becoming the most powerful. Every branch of our military has a special forces division; our schools should be as equally prepared. Thus, it is clear to me that we need a panel of trained teachers who can spot, help, and mentor the kids who will inevitably be left behind. That we allow millions to drop by the wayside is an indictment on our society.

It all begins with the subjects we teach. Any successful adult knows that motivation, inspiration, and knowledge are needed before anything is ever accomplished. It is a miracle that children who have not been encouraged through the school system still have become the most successful individuals in society. The hard way lacks compassion and love. It is of the upmost necessity that we imbue our children in schools with the proper ideas and the proper mindset to be successful. With the right classes being taught in schools early enough, then the children will be encouraged to take on more difficult coursework, which includes the hard sciences.

After graduation, they will be better suited for the real-life obstacles that life presents. Year after year, student after student, one pertinent question is often asked without a satisfactory answer, "Why do I need to learn art, Spanish, chemistry, algebra, dance class, band, etc?" Somehow, I believe that the secret is out, that schools have chosen to teach classes and subjects that are not a necessity to success in life. What would better serve students in their future endeavors—learning how to bust a move; learning to say "Hola, mi nombre es Juan"; learning the formula for salt; learning the balance of a chemical equation; knowing the elements of a periodical table; or mastering the activities of daily living, principles of success, public speaking, interpersonal and team building, mental health, balancing a checkbook, budgets, and life skills? I am not proclaiming that it has to be one or the other, but I am challenging the choice of subjects being taught versus those that have been left out by academia. It's time to have a national debate involving children, teachers, and parents concerning what is taught in elementary, junior high school, and high school.

I can remember being in the fourth grade and having a speech impediment. I had to appear in Mrs. Lamondo's office every Tuesday afternoon during lunchtime. Yes, for one hour per week, I had to be reminded that I had a speech impediment that was caused by being born in a Latin American country. There is a story that Associate Justice of the Supreme Court Sonia Sotomayor was having difficulties in her English class due to her Hispanic background, and the interpretation of both cultures was creating confusion for her. Personally speaking, speech class had such a damaging effect on my self-esteem. It had a zero-sum positive effect on my ability to pronounce words. Imagine, out of 300 children in those classes, four of us had to separate from the rest of the kids to head to speech therapy. Then we rejoined them after lunch. My classmates believed that we must be modified, slower than the rest of them, which translated into having lesser intelligence. My upbringing was fraught with failure. Without Pierre's box, I believe I would now be in a potter's field.

It was Anthony Santiago, Maria Carmoza, John Gonzalez, and I who would be required to meet at 12:30 p.m. We were chosen because our grades were low and could not pronounce basic words in class. The kids who had good pronunciation would be able to play out in the field. James Earl Jones would have been sitting between Anthony and me. The four of us would sit in her office and follow her instructions, as we watched the regular kids run around and kick the soccer balls across the field. Often the speech instructor would leave us alone in the class and Anthony and I would do wrestling moves on each other. Why is it that sometimes educators are the biggest deterrent to a child's educational development? Didn't she realize the obvious, that part of my inability to pronounce certain words was because I was from a Latin American country? Every time I was about to speak, I would confuse English words with Spanish words. To this day, there are still a handful of words that will not roll off my tongue.

When all was said and done, my speech impediment was not cured at that juncture. Mrs. Lamondo signed off on us, and we all moved on to the next grade and so did our "speech impediments." Today Anthony is a famous comedian, Maria is a professor at New York University, John has served his country honorably in the military, and I am a successful trial lawyer. Speech therapy was consequently banned the following year after our guinea pig experiment was over. Someone must have figured out that the speech therapy was futile, given their approach to the problem.

I did resolve 90 percent of my speech impediment, 10 years later. I solved it by avoiding what I was incapable of pronouncing. I used a great book called a thesaurus. There are words that I will never be able to pronounce. The Spanish say that certain words should roll right off of your tongue. I was unable to pronounce and deliver certain words, so what I did was study the synonyms. Problem solved! Why was the educational system unable to help me during these vulnerable times? I had friends with dyslexia who went undiagnosed for years.

Somehow, I was able to survive until I met my first mentor in life. After that, life was no longer an impossible riddle, but many obstacles that were conquerable. One cannot survive without the right mentors, be they parents, teachers, life coaches, or pastors.

Chapter 5

*If the blind put their hands in God's, they find their
way more surely than those who see but have not
faith or purpose.*

—Helen Keller

L ooking back at my life since the time that I
was in high school is rather daunting. The
only thing I can compare it to is when I rode my
motorcycle at high speeds and everything to the
left and everything to the right of me was just a
blur. I glanced at everything for a second, then
new objects would rapidly appear in front of me.
Meeting Pierre thirty years ago seems like just an
illusion, graduating from Stony Brook University
and the University of Chicago School of Law was
just a fleeting moment, although at the time it felt
like an eternity! Becoming an assistant district
attorney in Brooklyn and then starting my own
law firm. Wow, more than one could believe, but
those times are behind me forever.

I wish to share with you another note that was left to me from Pierre. It concerns the rapidity of life.

> *Death is eventual, in death everything stops,*
> *do not slow down in life while you are alive,*
> *smelling the fragrance of a rose*
> *only takes a moment.*

It felt just like yesterday, when I was accepted to law school. Those were the times that I was sleeping in my Volkswagen, the times that I was homeless, however, it never disturbed me. Correct, sleeping in my car, showering at the local gym, and attending classes seemed normal to me at the time. The mind is a lot stronger than we give it credit! Moving to Brooklyn from Chicago was a real transition, but it finally made me a stabilized member of society. From that time onward I was able to forge ahead, meeting Nadira and practicing all the principles of success given to me as a young man.

Nadira and I lived the perfect love affair for over twenty years. Who would have believed meeting someone on the subway could turn out to be an everlasting love? Often, I sit in my attic with my cup of tea and ask myself, "Why wasn't I told by

Pierre how quickly time elapses? Was that part of his second box, the one on heavenly success?"

It feels like Nadira and I met just yesterday, but it has been over two decades. My wife is old now, and she's not doing well. It is time for me to stop these moot contemplations and tend to her dinner.

"Nadira, wake up, its already 7:00 a.m." She pivots her head and tries to act like she is surprised with my announcement. As I assist her out of the king-size bed, she tells me about her hunger pangs. "I know, darling." She smiles, just wanting to be acknowledged by me.

Many people have looked at me over the years and have shown empathy for me because of how I take care of her needs. The public sees it like a burden; I see it as an act of love. How could any act of love be a burden? I am in good company, the most beloved person in the Catholic church, the pope, washes the feet of those people who are less important than he. It was Jesus who started this tradition. It truly is an honor to serve a person or a country one loves. Burden should only apply for trivial and useless acts.

Nadira and I follow a regular schedule. I am really lucky because when I go to the gym with her, I have a personal trainer who watches her in the pool, while

I run 15 miles on the treadmill, and, yes, I have it set on a ten-level incline. After the gym and the daily food shopping, we are back home again, joined at the ankles, hips, and shoulders.

Slowly, you learn that a decade is like a year, a year is like a month, a month is like a week and a week is like a second! You blink and you're old. At times you are looking at life, let's say age twenty-three, and you feel depressed about not having a career, a home, a relationship. Then before you know, it is your fiftieth birthday. Soon you want to know, "Who ran the fifty-yard dash on my last fifty years!" Ask anyone over forty. It sometimes feels like a prank. The joke is on anyone who doesn't value each day—each minute. Failure stabs you in the back, not straight on. It slowly lulls you into a stage of comfort, until you have lost your inquisitive curiosity for success.

Nadira is now in that king-size bed. Lucky for her that years back I gained a fascination for cooking and, of course, once I get into a new hobby I obsess over it until I master it. Moreover, having reprogrammed my way of thinking empowered me even more. Learning to cook like a French chef was no different for me than learning to fly a single-engine Cessna 172, writing books, or passing the bar exam. The same tools to accomplish one are used to accomplish the others. Once you learn this nugget of wisdom, you can have fun accomplishing the weirdest things, like when I learned how to speak Mandarin, just so that I could go to Chinatown and interact with the local merchants. Cantonese was limited to Hong Kong, so I didn't learn that dialect.

When it comes to all the gourmet meals I have mastered, I can immediately recall every herb, spice, or condiment. Who would have thought that the kid who was such a picky eater would be so acquainted with so many recipes as an adult? It's more than just healthy, organic food; it's more than just another hobby when I prepare a chili, a paella, an Indian curry or any other dish from forty different countries. It gives me a tribal link to the people from all those cultures. Somehow I knew a decade ago that Nadira would need for me to have this survival skill, the ability to prepare her nourishment . . . to lessen her suffering. It was inventor Thomas Edison who once stated to a reporter in 1902, "The doctor of the future will give no medicine but will interest his patients in the care of the human frame, in diet and in the cause and prevention of disease." Simplicity is genius.

My dad, Cesar, would often say to me that some things only make sense when they are applied at the right moment and not necessarily when you learn them. I always observed him as the greatest gentleman who roamed the earth.

It's odd how Nadira is now fifty-six years old, but she looks like the day I met her on Queens Blvd., she looks twenty-five! To me, I see her at twenty-five years old. How is it that I don't see her advanced age? I once read a medical study performed on 760 married couples over a twenty-year span, and it concluded that couples who met when they were young in life *always* remember the other person as if they were in their youth; it's a phenomenon that can't be explained but one that is true with us. She is my Mona Lisa. I will never see age seventy, eighty, or beyond!

At fifty-two years of age, I appear to be in my twenties. I believe that it is due to good genes and the five health habits that I have religiously applied throughout the past decade. Those habits of health were taught to me by an endearing women from Vietnam who was 103 years old. Looking at her birth certificate, I feared for its preservation, not hers. It had many more years on it than she did, even the government stamp was no longer legible.

On the rare occasions when Nadira and I go to a restaurant, I am asked for identification. Imagine being more than three decades over the legal drinking limit and still being questioned about your age.

I retired from the law, not because I am old or weak, but because I felt there was nothing else to accomplish, to achieve, or no other worthy battles to engage in. As a young man, after studying and applying the life principles given to me by Pierre, I entered the world with no limitations, no fears, and no reservations about the goals I was going to accomplish. What I never envisioned was that everything in life has a finish line. There is a beginning and an end to all matters and that applied to my career. I no longer wish to stand on the top of that mountain. Notice the only difference between me at twenty-five and me at fifty-two is *my desire, not what the world desires for me.*

Yes, it is a such a lucrative business, I quit at the peak of my reputation, so states my Google representative and my Google rankings. My phone still rings, people still email and text me, asking if I would step in and salvage their life. Meaning that their loved one is in a dire circumstance and they need a miracle man, me. I tell them, "Look for a life coach, another great lawyer, a pastor, or a counselor. Sorry, I am no longer taking any more criminal cases." I think to myself, *I am finished. I don't feel the passion I had when I was twenty-eight.* I recall watching movies and TV series on these heroic characters in the courtroom. I wanted to be the hero in people's lives. As is often said, be careful what you wish for!

Heroism is often unrewarding. For most individuals, it should remain in movies and comic books. I now believe that each person should be the hero of his or her own destination. As sports great Dave Winfield once stated, "You know, heroes are ordinary people that have achieved extraordinary things in life." I was under-ordinary and below-ordinary, according to my teachers, but then I wasn't.

Now that my career is behind me, I only wish to be with Nadira, Dante, and my God. Yes, Dante, my 210-pound Dogue de Bordeaux that is 80 percent human and 10 percent canine. I have no idea what his other 10 percent is, but I think feline. I would like to settle back in life now without feeling a responsibly to humankind. Is that too much to ask? Did I not achieve and share enough in my life? Why do I feel like Jonah? The Jonah who spent three days and three nights in the belly of the whale. Yes, that Jonah . . . the one who was asked by God to travel to Nineveh and deliver a message! I am starting to see the rationale of the other half of the dream I had 20 years ago . . . the school and the prison.

It's 10:00 p.m. I can't sleep; watching the news is not an option, it stopped being the news and has become propaganda. The anchors have proven that they only have one mission . . . to indoctrinate their audiences. Ok, I am painting a broad brushstroke, but most people agree with me in whole. So 67 percent of Americans, according to a recent Gallup poll, concluded that most Americans are engaging more often in social media than with traditional media. After walking away from my business, it was easy for me to gravitate toward social media because of the individual personal opinions and unfiltered information that were being provided. As usual, at midnight, I climbed into bed and went to sleep with the only person I have ever slept with in the past twenty-five years.

And again, like the timing of a clock, the next day I am back online with over 18,000 followers on the three major social media companies. I bounce from one company to another so that I can engage with various demographics, ages, and different political affiliations. Facebook is by far the platform where the questions and answers are never boring, and that's phrasing it mildly. Often my page becomes like an open therapy session with hundreds of therapists sharing advice, love, and support to the person in need.

My forum on Facebook is about asking deep, challenging questions to the public, questions that have never been asked in an open forum and discussed in the same manner. Every night I pose the nightly question and within minutes, responses flood my page. The other interesting aspect is that there are thousands of people with popcorn in hand just reading the back and forth colloquy between the participants and me. I know, because I have been stopped hundreds of time on the streets from people who follow me, and they all mention how intriguing the questions have been, yet none of these people ever answered a single one of my last 700 questions.

Sometimes I will ask a question that compels the majority to answer with no response needed from me. My technique of asking the most potent question is based on my theory that the question must put the reader between a rock and a hard place! The spectrums of questions I ask my audience are broad, from "What would you do if this were the last day of your life?" to "Tell me how online dating is working for you as opposed to your traditional dates?" Those questions seem fairly straightforward but you would be amazed on that second question how many women replied that they were raped by someone they met online. Everything and anything is up for discussion.

Often, the people who follow me on any of my social media platforms will reach me personally and ask for my opinion about personal matters. About 25 percent of the questions I am asked are based on the dilemmas that people posed to me in my emails. Oddly enough, many people want me to pose the questions anonymously in a public forum, so that they can get feedback from hundreds of people throughout all walks of life. Every day in my inbox, I receive information or questions about suicide, depression, infidelity, cheating, and incest.

The truth is that when I first started to participate in forums on social media, I didn't take it seriously, as most people seemed to just want to argue about any subject, ranging from love to the apocalypse. However, there are specific forums on war veterans, suicide prevention, daily inspiration, and the likes where you will encounter real love and helpful information being shared. As has been stated, "It takes a village . . . "

In the past couple of years, my eyes have been opened to a world of people who I would never have encountered. Whether they are sitting in their homes, their jobs, or at the local Starbucks, they feel that they have some level of privacy answering my questions, or maybe they don't care anymore. I have used social media to give the public a way to confess and express their suffering in life. *A way for them to express themselves in a deeply private way and have someone listen . . . for once!* Somehow, when I pose a question, people on social media are quick to respond with some real painful truths.

Imagine this, I have asked this question, "What event made you lose faith in humankind?" You would not believe how many people have lost their children, spouses, or have lost their entire family in one tragic event. Was it always this way? **How did I not see so much human suffering** prior to engaging on social media! I no longer mock these public forums! Did my "little world" insulate me from the suffering of normal folks? Had I forgotten the gift I was given and sinned by not paying it forward?

Its Friday night, 11:35 p.m., and I sip on my best Kentucky Bourbon. Granted, when I was a trial lawyer, I drank expensive batches, but honestly I can't tell the difference anymore. Maybe it's just rationalization of the brain. Rationalization of the brain? You know like settling for something because it's the only option you believe is available. Even in marriages, I have witnessed rationalization of the brain. I know it's not proper English, but I love when something just makes sense but it is stated incorrectly. Or is it that I am rebelling against my sixth grade grammar teacher, Mr. Subbert? The night seems like it will end like every other night for the past twenty-four months, until I open my Facebook Messenger account and read the following: "Please contact Cynthia. She's on Facebook, forty-two years old, depressed, lives alone, and I think she's gonna take her life!"

I sent her five messages from 11:30 to 1:00 a.m. with no response. All of my messages to her indicated that I intended to form a friendship with her, if she permitted. For the next five days, I looked for Cynthia but was unable to find her, until one day I found more information on her friend who initially reached out to me. Automatically, I went into high gear with everything that made me a shark killer in the courtroom. The conversation went as follows.

Me: "Hi, this is Walter, you left . . . "

Him: "Yes, thank you, sir, for trying to reach Cynthia. I just brought her back home from the hospital. She is still alive. I found her in her room still breathing."

Me: "Please forward me her info. I would like to visit today or tomorrow."

Him: "Ok, by the way, I am Norman. I have been following everything you post on Facebook! Don't you ever run out of crazy questions to ask? I wish I had your type of knowledge so this wouldn't have happened to Cynthia! I have followed you and have witnessed the way you change the negativity and anger in people."

Me: "What is your connection to her . . . how do you know her?"

Him: "We served in the Marines. She was badly hurt in Iraq, and I was on the front line to extract her from the enemy combatants."

Me: "God bless you, and thank you for your service! Send me her info, please."

On the following day, Nadira and I drove to Natick, Massachusetts, where Cynthia lived with her mother. It's crazy that strangers can love each other without knowing each other. We spent the whole day with them and, when we left her, I felt that we had accomplished what we went there for. Cynthia had the most beautiful Labrador Retriever on this planet. I think he knew that I was her spiritual doctor, because he licked and kissed my hand throughout my stay.

Every day after that visit with Cynthia, she was always the first person to answer any of the questions I posted for that day, and not with a yes or a no, but with a long-ass narrative. I cherished it each time.

On August 6, 2021, at 10:07 p.m., I received another message from Norman. He indicated he knew someone by the name of Tony who wanted to take his own life.

Chapter 6

Moby Dick seeks thee not. It is thou, thou,
that madly seekest him!

—Herman Melville

Norman had served his third tour of duty with Cynthia, when she was injured in the war against Iran and Russia in 2019. Her respiratory system was highly compromised due to the nerve gas released in a government building that she was clearing for the rest of the team. Norman once stated to me that he wanted to "save lives," as I had done for Cynthia and Tony, no longer with guns but through ideas.

I walked away from him and told him that all the people who I had counseled for the past two years were not planned, but more spontaneous. I told him it happened because I had retired and that at the time I did not take social media seriously. My deep discussions with real people were not foreseeable to me at the time! I also told Norman that I had lost interest in engaging so many people on social media with all their problems.

It never dawned on me that people who were suicidal, going through a wicked divorce, or were just plain depressed needed someone to assist them to some safe ground in such a public way. How selfish of me not to realize that people who were hurting would take any assistance that they could get. Somehow, I became that person, that counselor . . . unbeknownst to me.

Next time I saw Norman was on July 31, 2019. I came home, and he was having Darjeeling tea with my wife, Nadira. When I entered the house, she said to me, "If I didn't know any better, he could be our son!" Game over, Nadira and I had a seventeen-year-old son named Marco, who was killed in a car accident due to a driver who had consumed alcohol and fentanyl. The intoxicated driver collided with Marco head-on, and he stood no chance of survival.

It was I who inspired Marco to save his money for a car, to get his junior license and apply early. Nadira, like any protective mother, disagreed with me that he should be on the road at such an early age. She was the one who received the call from the Suffolk County Police Department that our son was deceased. I think she immediately went into a deep depression, not only because she adored him, what I call "agape love," but because it meant to her that my love affair with her would not be perpetuated by our son and his future wife. It would end with us! Nadia and I even joked on several occasions that Marco would meet a young lady named Sharon. We always said that they would meet in an unsuspecting place, like on an New York City subway train, a Greyhound bus terminal, or some mangy manger location.

That dream is no more.

Every week for the past twenty years, I had visited the scene where his life was taken from him to place flowers and to speak to my only son. Driving to Horseblock Road in Farmingville weekly was the only secret I ever kept from Nadira. Marco was a beautiful, loving, God-fearing, young athlete who had everything parents could ask for. At birth, no one would have predicted that he would have turned out to be such a beast in sports; he was short, had bad vision, and was anemic! I remember him saying to me after his first wrestling competition, "Dad, knowing that no one believes in me, except you and Mom, somehow makes me want to fight harder."

I really think after Marco's death Nadira wasn't strong enough to accept the cruel hands of life. Her recent diagnosis . . . her lack of memory changed how I answered her every day. I was much softer toward her, like how I responded to her. In the past when she said something that wasn't supported by facts, I would go into cross-examination mode, now she says the strangest things and all I do is kiss her forehead. I think she sometimes makes things up to see if I will change my tactics. She keeps a poker face without, but I know that within she is giggling at me, knowing that I can't correct her.

Now watching Nadira speaking with Norman, I can't interrupt or challenge her on the statement that Norman has similarities to our deceased son. After all this time of being around Norman, I never picked up those coincidental character traits, but Nadira did! Maybe it is because her life is winding down and there is no room in the heart for frivolous thoughts unlike the rest of us. It is only now that it is obvious to me.

I excused myself from Nadira and took Norman by the hand to the attic. This is where I kept all of my writings, my antique firearms, my photos, and the personal valuables that I had accumulated over my lifetime. His eyes were wide open, staring at the photos on the wall showing me with what most of society would call famous people.

I asked him to go through the hundreds of photos that I had and pick out the best one, the most impressive one. He seemed so eager to do this. He said, "This player is in the Baseball Hall of Fame . . . that's Roy Campanella!" I responded by taking the card out of his hand and commenced to light a match to it. He looked at me like I had just taken food away from a homeless person. He knew that I could get about $25,000 at auction for the authenticity of that signed card. Do you wish to now really learn what is more valuable than all these items? He was still contemplating the destruction of that valuable idol.

"Norman, you have continued to seek me out. I am here for you, and I now recognize that we meant for a higher calling. Are you willing to come over every day, so that I can explain to you the greatest worldly gift that I have ever received? It was given to me in a box with no real instructions and in an unorganized manner. Based on the content of that box I received decades ago, I was able to determine the seven principles in life needed to succeed, without fail.

"I will give you the seven lessons that were hidden in that box that I have used in my life to overcome all of my deficits and handicaps. Over the years of application, these principles have become muscle memory for me, thus I have stopped thinking about the principles and just found myself acting as if they were ingrained in my DNA. The key is to practice each principle as if you were practicing any other action in your life, then if you find yourself in a highly stressful or competitive environment, the principle needed for that circumstance will become your ammunition.

"The most difficult part for me was when I first started applying the lessons on my own. I had no proof of their benefits. *Faith is essential*. You, on the other hand, have me as an example of a person who has lived by these belief systems and has succeeded on multiple fronts. If I told you all of the things that I have accomplished in a short life, you would be in disbelief. If I told you where I started in life, as opposed to where I ended in life, you would again be in disbelief.

"Know this, these lessons have been applied for thousands of years before modern-day scientists and psychiatrists decided to place labels on them. Today, you can turn to any television channel, read any blog or book, and you will find these beliefs scattered in an unorganized fashion like a bunch of puzzle pieces that have yet to be joined. Additionally, scientists and the so-called experts are now complicating them with technical jargon."

 I paused and then I continued. "I have a question for you, Norman. Does ten hours a day for three days feel like too much of a commitment?"

He responded without hesitation. "It seems too little, not enough time to learn such things that can change one's life forever!"

I was pondering whether I should do any further explanation, given all that I had just said. "Oh, my dear friend, after those thirty hours of lecture, you will spend the rest of your life applying these principles and conquering the implausible." My words seemed to start sink in. "Get a good night's rest. Meet me in my attic at 5:50 a.m."

As we stood and headed toward the front door, Norman asked, "Why 5:50 a.m?

I looked over at him and said, "Because at 5:45 a.m. every morning, the Canadian geese pass over my neighborhood. To me, hearing the honking of that flock is equivalent to listening to the great composer Lang Lang play 'Ave Maria' on the piano."

Chapter 7

The only true wisdom is in knowing
you know nothing.

—Socrates

The next day, Nadira intercommed me while I was completing my first life's lesson for Norman. "Sweetheart, that young man is sitting on our stoop, just sitting, pointing his flashlight in the dark." I pressed the button on my watch to illuminate the time. I have always sat in our dim attic room when I was thinking or meditating on ideas or solutions; maybe I am nocturnal and so are the solutions because we both favor silence and twilight.

I replied to the intercom, "Its 3:20 a.m. our sit-down is not scheduled for another two hours. I am heading down." As I stand and head out of the boxy room, I half stumble over Dante . . . he doesn't budge, snoring like an old man who drank a bottle of Jack Daniel's, not what one would expect from the protector of the family . . . a Dogue de Bordeaux. He gave me that look like "Really, you didn't notice me?" I pet him, like I pet Nadira, neither finds it insulting.

I prepared the daily, black coffee; opened the door; and signaled for Norman to enter. He does so with little confidence. "Kid, thank you for being so early!" With a note of levity and in rhetorical fashion, I asked, "Who taught you lesson six already?" He smiled and we proceeded to sit next to each other and sip on the coffee that I had just brewed.

Our tutorial moments began.

"Here is your notepad. We will be done with these first three lessons in about ten hours and I will cover Slate 1 through Slate 3. When you return tomorrow, we will cover Slates 4, 5, and 6. On the third and final day we will cover Slate 7.

"The refrigerator is to your left, there will be five water bottles each day, so that you can stay hydrated. By the bay windows, you have coffee pods, so feel free to fuel yourself if your attention span starts to wane. Also, as far as food is concerned, it's either tuna fish or a sardine sandwich each day with a slice of avocado. If you wish to have an early dinner, then I will intercom Nadira for that. You are not going to leave the room except for bathroom breaks. Any questions, my friend?"

Never saying a word, I could tell by his

descriptive brown face that he now understood that I had thrown the gauntlet to the ground.

"I will first point out to you a weakness that exists in all humans."

He appeared rather offended at these opening lines. Looking somewhat prideful, he tilted his head back but didn't comment. I picked up on this human fault and commented, "Even someone like you, Norman, who has been trained and disciplined by the US military, has not been given all the training necessary for this unpredictable life, this life that has even confounded the Albert Einsteins of this world."

"*Please don't fall prey to the misnomer that having a weakness means that a person is weak.* On the other hand, if weaknesses are discovered early enough, then the necessary adjustments can be made so that change and then ultimately growth can occur. In every new endeavor, whether it is in the form of martial arts, piloting a plane, or becoming an expert in any career, there is a set of principles that will allow you to succeed and advance over others. The challenges of life require a game plan, a predetermined set of rules, a playbook that was spoken, written, and tested by the predecessors before us. Reinventing the wheel is a form of idiocy.

"So, Norman, in each lesson I will discuss and expose inherent weaknesses in most humans. After raising the red flags for you, we will then move on and discuss the remedy, this is what I labeled the slates! There are seven of them in total. Each slate is a necessary rule that is needed for humans to incorporate into their lives to fix those ingrained weaknesses. Lastly, I will pose several questions that relate directly to each slate. These questions can be answered by any one, and most people will have some similar responses for most of the questions, however, some questions call for an introspection of the soul.

"You don't know much about my past career, but I spent over two decades cross-examining expert witnesses, lay witnesses, and eyewitnesses. I have an infinity for questions, the right ones that elicit the right answers. When one *masters the skill of asking the right questions,* then one is closer than ever to resolving the dilemmas. Empowerment precedes the right questions asked.

"Never make a decision without asking as many questions that come to your mind about the problem at hand. Anyone who studies Einstein will see that this was one of his greatest skills. This is why the best life coaches are invaluable and are sought out by the wealthy. Think about that: CEOs, presidents, doctors, and lawyers seek a one-on-one with life coaches every day. Yet a mere thirty years ago the life coaches didn't exist. Yes, correct, necessity is the mother of invention. Why shouldn't a child, the poor, and the motivated have the same guidance? Life coaches have mastered a skill on the level of the most effective and prominent trial lawyers. *Learning how to ask the $64,000 question, over and over again. It is the beginning of all understanding!"*

Slate 1: The Empty Slate

Today is a new day that should not have any attachments or anchors to your past. First, if you start a new day thinking about *yesterday's problems,* you are already waking up with a thousand-pound gorilla on your back. Second, you have to accept that if you wish to advance further in your career, then you will need to let go of *your past and your present belief systems,* if they are not consistent with the seven slates of success. It's more likely that currently you do not have any principles that you rely on to overcome career obstacles.

There is also a chance that you have been functioning on some worthless ideas that were implanted in you by negative influences in your childhood. They cling to our brains like amoebas. Time to detach yourself from most of these parasites. Time to be open and embrace new ideas and techniques that have produced the most successful people in history. This requires trust and faith, the same trust and faith that I had when I was first given that magical box from Pierre. Again, consider these two notions.

1. Each new day should start with a rebirth.
2. Reject your past; it is an illusion.

All the principles in these lectures are based on these bedrocks. Today, you will stop repeating your past actions; they have handicapped you since childhood. *Practice every day stepping out of that box.* It is correct that we are born with certain traits, and if they are not reversed through repeated actions and through proper mentoring, then they will lead to our demise.

It's best if I now give you real-life examples so that you can connect the theories with the practical applications. In mentoring and coaching individuals, I have witnessed that the majority of people know some of the theories of success, but when I ask them some questions on the applications of those theories, few can explain. Even fewer of those people can give me an example of how they applied any principle of success to their careers. There is a major disconnect between the theory, how it generally applies in life, and how, if ever, they have applied it in their lives.

Here is your first real example that I submit to you. If you attempted to become a Navy SEAL, you would learn on day one that the first phase of frog training is the most difficult one. It is only eight weeks long, however two out of three candidates surrender. They call this "ringing the bell." It is usually the best athletes who do not survive this phase. The reason is because their slate is full of accomplishments, accolades, and egos. The US military intentionally created phase number one to *challenge your current belief system and the inner quitter in you!* And the ones who makes it past this phase exponentially have a higher chance to overcome the other phases.

Some people never learn how to get out of their own way; they hold on to their previous flawed belief systems. The military understands the voice that is heard by everyone faced with an unsurmountable task. The words sounds a lot like this, "This is too hard, this can't be done, this is not for me!"

Scenario number two is similar, but the challenges are different, thus I utilize it to drive home the point. If you receive an acceptance letter to law school, and you accept that challenge, you will be read the riot act on day one. The sum and substance of the inspirational introduction is as follows.

Welcome class of 2022. Congratulations, this is your dream . . . going to law school and one day making lots of money probably in a big civil lawsuit! It's the civil lawyers who ultimately get the big bucks! Or maybe you will represent that small percentage of innocent men who get acquitted and you will be seen as that heroic attorney in your community. Kinda like Atticus Finch in the fictional book written by Harper Lee, *To Kill a Mockingbird.* Some of you might even make it to the Supreme Court of the United States of America! Like Sonia Sotomayor, who is from Puerto Rican descendants and was born in the Bronx.

Now, for some reality! Look to the right of you. Now look to the left of you. One of you will not be here within four weeks. One of you will drop out, concede that the dream

was not meant to be. Now again, look around at all the students in this auditorium, half of them will despise the law within ten years after graduating from law school; they will live a life of misery. Now look just at the person next to you, look at each other, one of you will be an alcoholic before you retire from this prestigious profession called the law. Divorce, bankruptcies, suicides—we have it all for those of you who wish to join this prestigious membership.

Now take a look at the exit doors! It's still not too late. Make up your mind. If you still believe that this is your childhood dream, you are sorely mistaken, lawyering is similar to carrying the cross for a better cause or joining the special forces in the military . . . you will not be compensated adequately! You now have been warned. Have a pleasant day, everyone.

You will also realize after the first full day of class that you are two weeks behind on all of the subject matter. The load of work in the first year of law school is insurmountable, that is part of the psychology of creating a successful lawyer. The instructors are trying to create an individual who can balance multiple dilemmas and tasks without being fully prepared.

The average, brilliant, college student wants control, wants to understand all the coursework. That method of memorization works in college but not in law school. It's impossible in year one of law school; no one can memorize all the material and case law in torts, contracts, civil procedure, property, criminal law, and constitutional law. You can now start to see how one needs a certain set of rules, a belief system, principles that can be applied under any and all challenges, if you will, on demand. What you were taught in your earlier years in life, by your teachers, friends, and parents, will probably be insufficient for future success, unless you were mentored by the few who understand the slates of success.

You must let go of your current belief system or modify your way of thinking with the ones in these lessons. There is a reason that you and I met. I would venture to say that it's because you wanted success to be part of your existence. Time to apply these lessons that have survived thousands of years. Before any student drops out of law school, this is the voice and the words that they should hear: "I will not give up, I will find a way to make it to the finish line, even if I graduate at the bottom of my class!"

The dropout rate for car sales agents is 67 percent according to the *Automotive News.* The reason is that the rejection rate in any sales field is extremely high. The most successful car salespeople understand the dynamics of rejection but also see the possibility in every potential client. Think about that! Knowing that almost everyone a salesperson meets will probably not purchase a vehicle, but at the same moment believe that each client has an interest to buy. Joe Girard sold 13,001 cars within fifteen years of working for Chevrolet. He was recognized in the *Guinness Book of World Records* for selling the greatest number of cars in a single year. His attitude about difficulties and rejections was summarized by his quote, "The elevator to success is out of order. You'll have to use the stairs . . . one step at a time."

According to the National Association of Realtors, 87 percent of all real estate agents fail in the first five years. In this industry, there is more movement, additional costs to the sales agent, and the rejection threshold is similar to car sales, thus the attrition rate is higher. However, the most successful agents in real estate make millions! "Ringing the bell" in real estate becomes real and happens fast for those who pursue this lucrative venture. Only the dogged type of individuals stick it out year after year, knowing that the real estate market will challenge the "inner quitter" in all of us.

Why do so many fail in these environments of law schools, special forces, sales, etc? I can poll any audience in the world over the age of forty and ask them to name the **reasons why they missed the mark in reaching their career goals.** Inevitably, whether they were applying to nursing school, performed standup comedy, or were studying engineering, they will all respond with the identical answer. Go ahead, ask your friends, your family, or any stranger the exact question as to why they did not reach their ultimate goals and you will see the exact same responses. That's the rationale of this belief system, so that you will not have to spend decades trying to figure out what works, what doesn't, and what to avoid in your life.

Here are the enemies, according to the public.

1. Self-esteem, shyness
2. Parents interfering
3. Lack of discipline, laziness
4. Fear, anxiety

5. Self-confidence

6. Bad decision-making

7. Self-abuse, addiction

These are the deadly seven. Read them to yourself, ingrain them in your mind, but above all never capitulate your life to them. Millions of people have lamented due the destruction that they have caused. They might not look intimidating at first glance, but don't take them lightly; they are the wolf in sheep's clothing. They end visions, they end childhood dreams, and they leave the masses miserable when they are done. Indicators are all around us, there are telltale signs when success and when failure are near. *To speak only about the principles of success and leave out the principles of failure is a fatal error.* Reject the deadly seven reasons that have just been discussed; they have destroyed millions of careers . . . and lives. Wherever you see or feel them around you, knock them down, plow or power through them.

Today, you will put aside your pride, your ego, and you will follow these principles in each endeavor you wish to pursue. This will place you in the arena of the non-dropouts. You will not accept that destiny assigned to those who are blindsided by failure. You are on notice that those around you will fail in education, work, competitions, and all aspects of life. Not you! You will hold the line in everything you wish to accomplish! *All failure is based on applying the wrong system to the challenges at hand.*

Failure is no longer a word that you will fear; on the other hand, when failure is presented, you will realize it is a challenge to apply one of the slates. Failure is more like a yield sign than it is a stop sign. You will learn how to *challenge failure instead of submitting to it.* Always remember that failure isn't stubborn and it wishes for you to tap out or submit early. It is more like a weak bully than a strong competitor. It chips away at your confidence and it needs you to agree. Sometimes it will take one great effort to accomplish your goals, and other times it will take several. None of that matters. What does matter is that you do not concede to failure's demand. *Failure fears the non-quitter and is friendly to the weak.*

Today, you are tearing down the idea of idols, and you are going to start constructing your own talents and your work ethics. To do this, you must take off the blindfolds. Your uniqueness! This is your gift: No one can duplicate you and surpass your individuality. If you practice the principles I have given to you and apply them in your way, with your voice, and with your mannerisms, then you will achieve what was meant for you in this short life. If you attempt to duplicate others, follow others, and capitulate to others in this world, you have given up your greatest strength. The combination of your uniqueness as an individual, coupled with the right manuscript for success, is what will allow you to advance in your chosen profession. *Love yourself enough, don't reject yourself . . . by following others.* Following others is a form of rejecting yourself. It was the famous, late, rock artist Chester Bennington from Linkin Park who sang out prophetic lyrics in his collaboration with Jay-Z in the song "Numb." "All I want to do is be more like me and be less like you!" That was his war cry before he left this earth.

Pierre once left me this note.

On your road to achievements, be mindful that your terrain and obstacles will be uniquely different from others

Questions

1. What are three principles of success?

2. What is one principle of success that you have applied in your career, school, or endeavors?

3. Who is the person who mentored you about the principles of success?

4. Do you think people like Steve Jobs, Jeff Bezos, and Elon Musk have certain principles of success that they live by?

Chapter 8

Stay away from negative people.
They have a problem for every solution.

—Albert Einstein

Growing up, I never looked or expected support from my family or teachers. Somehow I found it odd that other children sought that type of confirmation. I don't know why, but I never received any advice about how I should compete in any sports or study in any school. There is a term for people like me, it's called a "self-made" person, one who has not relied on institutions or people to mentor them through their journey.

It is my experience that only about 10 percent of all humans have this ability to succeed without outside influences. I think it is a genetic trait. All other humans need mentors, coaches, pastors, or teachers to assure that they will reach maximum success in life. However, to me it is clear that if I had met Pierre earlier in my life, it would have dramatically increased my chances of success earlier. To me that is not in dispute. We all need the "right guidance" and, unfortunately, as I stated in lesson one, sometimes those who are responsible to mentor us not only fail in their obligations, but help facilitate in our road to failure.

Think about this, in any soccer game played in England, Italy, France, or Spain, there are approximately thirty-thousand fans in attendance. In any National Football League game that is played in the US, the average fan attendance is about fifty thousand; the Super Bowl consistently gets about seventy-five thousand in attendance.

Now let's look at the people who are actually participating in playing the game. It is roughly five to twenty-five players on each team and that includes the roster. Is there any chance that those participating in the sport are seeking advice from their families, their friends, or the public about how he or she should play in the competition of their lives? That scenario is not likely, and if it did occur it would be an aberration. The winners know how to win, and they also have keen instincts about their survival, based on all their efforts prior to reaching this higher stage. They know that few people who are giving them advice about success have any skin in the game. Separating the "wheat from the chaff" is essential in survival.

Learn this skill early: The skill of listening to all the people who are willing to give advice to you and how you should distinguish the good advice from the superfluous. All the other gibberish and faulty advice should be taken to the shredder. Allowing yourself to be indiscriminately influenced by your friends, family, and strangers will potentially derail your career. It was Thomas Edison, the great American inventor, who once stated that he was glad that he was deaf in one ear, so he wouldn't have to listen to half the negativity from the naysayers. Even a trusted person in your inner circle can ill advise you. Learning when to take and accept good advice is worth noting.

I have taken over a dozen polls on this subject that have included more than 800 participants. The vast majority of people in these polls have concluded that their family and friends have detrimentally influenced them about their career choices. As shameful as that sounds, I can only report to you my findings.

Do not seek approval from others. On the other hand, asking opinions from others is a sign of intelligence. In the end, learn to listen to your own inner voice, as the consensus of the majority is way over-rated. These results do not mean that those individuals do not care about you; it means to be wary of the pitfalls inherent in free advice. Caveat, there are parents, spouses, partners, and friends who should be your best advisors. If you fit this category, then you already know that these people have your best interests at heart and that they have helped you succeed in the past. If you have a great relationship with your mother, father, friend, pastor, or any other mentor, then please heed their advice about moving forward with your career.

Anyone in your life can convince you of why you should not go after your goals in life! The reasons are endless and, in a way, they are often rationale, however, they don't take into account the human spirit and the human desire to overcome the odds. Many people who love you, give you "safe" advice about your career goals. What they don't consider is that you might be the person who will sacrifice yourself to reach that point that others will not. They are relying on the safe bet . . . not the exceptional.

Thus, they render reliable advice, not the type of advice that will challenge you to fail or succeed. In their minds, they see safety as the ultimate accomplishment. In their minds, because of their shortcomings, they see that the odds are against you, they themselves, might not have been challenged to their full potential. Or maybe the challenges that they experienced vary greatly from yours. That's pragmatic! That's reasonable, *but it does not contemplate the exceptional efforts that you might be able to deliver!*

Slate 2: Time to Reprogram

Recognize, for the first time in your life, that your insecurities, the way you think about life might have its roots way back to the beginning of your childhood. For most of us, it does. Anyone can be conditioned to be afraid, to have low-self-esteem, and to not take risks. Our natural instinct is to avoid risk, that is ingrained in all humans. But the fear ingrained in our genes thousands of years ago is not relevant to our survival today. Because times are different, because circumstances are different, we can now adjust to the challenges of modern society, risk taking today is different from the risk taking during the Triassic and Jurassic periods. As humans, we will have to reprogram our minds to not see risk taking as a decision of finality. It no longer is; however, our systems are programmed to see failures as the elimination of our beings.

Most people do not capture their dreams, attain the right profession, or surpass their own expectations. This is due to the negativity in their minds and the negativity freely spread by others. It's based on fear of failure, which is interpreted in our minds as the risk of life. Once we can understand that our ingrained instincts are betraying us on the issue of risk taking, then we will be free to venture out and succeed, fail, or try again. Do not fault yourself for feeling anxious about risk taking, fault yourself if you do not realize that risk taking does not equal the end of your life or death as it did millions of years ago. Acknowledge the following: *Negativity spurns fear. Fear gives birth to excuses. Excuses are not based on reality.*

It all starts at childhood and continues throughout adulthood.

Psychologist Paul Ekman and others prominent in their field have agreed that humans have a small group of innate emotions, fear is one of them. This goes back millions of years. One who is afraid will also have anxiety. Back to the issue of being rational, most fears are irrational, no real basis for its existence other than what was ingrained in our genes long ago. Moreover, in our childhood, these fears were nurtured, fed, and condoned. When we were young, they need to be replaced by rationality, they need to be confronted, or else they take on a life of their own. If fear of facing a bully, giving a class speech, or asking someone out on a date is not squashed early on in life, then eventually it festers and ultimately becomes a hang-up at the least, a character trait at worse.

Rationality gets developed by practicing the principles of success. Again, rationality gets developed by practicing the principles of success. No one is born with rationality in a world full of influences and fear. As an example, if you had a fear as a child of drowning, then that would be a good moment for a mentor to show you how to dispel it. Your fears as a child do not have to travel into your adulthood, and, unfortunately often they do because they have not been properly sought out. That is the most profound and liberating statement one can receive. Let me phrase that differently. *What you are today, does not have to be what you will be tomorrow.* Believe me, when I tell you, that no matter what your past mistakes have been and no matter what wayward life you have lived, it does not prevent a new sunrise in your life. That is the promise we get when we rise every morning. You, and only you, can reject the new day and harken for yesterday to rejoin you.

For better or worse, there are countless experiments in history that demonstrate what is known as classical conditioning. In essence, this is where you condition people to act in a way they normally wouldn't. Even though in today's standards, these experiments would be considered unethical and illegal, when they were conducted there was nothing preventing their practice. One of the most famous studies was published for the world to see. In 1920, the *Journal of Experimental Psychology* published what was called the "Little Albert experiment."

The goal of the experiment was to create or condition a phobia in a stable child. Prior to the experiment, the child had no fear, no issues, and no phobia with a certain object. After the experiment, the child was emotionally unstable with that certain object. The child in the experiment was exposed to a domesticated white rat; the child played with it, petted it, and was comfortable with the rat. It was assumed that to the child the rat was a furry, harmless toy. The experimenters would allow the child to play with the white, furry animal for short periods of time.

At some juncture, the experimenters started making loud noises when the furry, white pet was allowed to stay with the child, thus, the child started equating the loud noise with the white rat, because that was the only time the noise was played. At some point, the child started to cry every time he was introduced to the white rat.

The next part of the experiment was when the experimenters brought out not the white rat, but other furry animals, such as a white rabbit. The child would immediately start to get emotional and cry until the new, furry, white creature was removed. It was learned that Albert, the child, would cry when seeing objects such as a white rabbit, a furry dog, and white cotton on a mask. The child was now conditioned to believe that the white, furry object was the threat, the reason for the loud noise, and the child would never venture toward that object.

As psychiatrist Karl Menninger taught us, "Fears are educated into us, and can, if we wish, be educated out." This is what our early experiences have taught us, and they often train us to fear things with no real rationality. When we have that fear, it prevents us from taking risks, from rejection, from attempting the unknown. Thus we find a safe zone, a comfort zone, comfortable, based on our childhood conditioning, and, sadly, we often do not recognize how we have certain traits that will affect our chances of successful careers. It's time to fix fear and negative programming.

You will find that risk taking can't be avoided in the pursuit of winning. To be a risk taker, one needs to conquer doubt. But I have discovered that too many people make too much out of their doubt and their risk taking. I have also discovered that the people who lack in both risk taking and conquering doubt, is not because they are not prepared and not intelligent enough to succeed, but because of the following four obstacles.

1. Over-thinking the challenge
2. Ego
3. Fear
4. Low self-esteem

Programming is involved in creating these obstacles in a person's mind, that is, from your experiences and interactions with the world growing up.

It is clear throughout human competitions that the race doesn't go to the swiftest, the most popular, or the fan favorite, but to the *one who takes the necessary steps, one by one, day by day, in the pursuit of the victory* . Let go of your ego, it is a one-thousand pound gorilla with no pound of worth. Program your mind daily. Program it by seeking challenges in life, which could be at the gym working out, on a school assignment, or any other endeavor.

Now, program your mind to see defeat differently. You accomplish this by taking on any challenges that are in front of you. You do this so that you can feel how it is to not win in everything that you undertake. If someone is at a local park playing a game a chess, sit down and play against them, although the odds of winning are small. Condition out of your system that not winning is failing. If you only participate in the things that you are good at, you will never program your mind to ignore failure. Ignoring failure when it happens is a prerequisite to attaining your highest goals.

Pierre was much more eloquent than I when he left this note for me.

> *When you unmask defeat, you will not see the face of failure.*

As you can imagine, there are many traits that you will need to reprogram. When you no longer view a defeat as a failure, then you are on your way to many more victories on this journey of success. Enjoy the irony of that last statement. Detaching the myth—that defeat and failure are not remotely related—is a concept that will draw confusion from many. Keeping them connected will create more failure than success. Separate them and distance them until there is no connection.

When you become that person who unmasks Mr. Failure's real face, you will start to understand the empowerment of the seven slates of success. As of today, fear will not stop you from failing or winning, these outcomes are shared by all winners. The only real loser is the one who doesn't stand up to the odds or the challenges before them.

So, you now know what defines failure. *Failure is defined by not trying. Moreover, your self-esteem and your confidence is handmade by taking on the challenge.* It is not made by losing the challenge. Winning alone is not enough. If it were, all champions would have low self-esteem, because no one is undefeated in life. No one! Name one.

Babe Ruth, arguably the best baseball player of all times, hit 714 home runs. The only two other players who surpassed his home runs were Barry Bonds and Hank Aaron. Ruth played in 1948! Bonds played in the 1990s, and Aaron played in the 1970s. So was Babe Ruth more of a winner than a loser? No, he led the American League as the "king of strikeouts" for five seasons. He had 1,330 strikeouts in his baseball career! So, statistically he struck out twice as much as he succeeded in batting. He's still the best, remember that.

Do not be so quick to judge a person who is currently on top of their game as a winner. Wait for the moment when they are de-elevated in their career to see if they are operating under these beliefs system. Cultivate the attitude of being the one who *dares to fail, but strives to win.* The sixteenth US president, Abraham Lincoln, operated under this belief system concerning his career goals. Think about how he felt when he went through the following "failures."

1. 1832—lost Illinois state election.
2. 1836—had a nervous breakdown.
3. 1838—lost election as Illinois House speaker.
4. 1843—lost run for US Congress.
5. 1854—lost election for US senator.
6. 1856—lost run for US vice president.
7. 1858—lost run for US senator.
8. 1860—elected US president

One of the greatest competitors once proclaimed, "I've missed over 9,000 shots in my career. I've lost almost 300 games. 26 times I've been trusted to take to the game-winning shot and missed. I've failed over and over and over again in my life. And that is why I succeed." That was spoken by a sports legend Michael Jordan.

Take a moment and think about the top three things that hurt you the most when you were young. For example, being left back from school, not getting into the college of choice, being passed up for a promotion, the person you loved left you, not making a sports team, a dishonorable discharge from the military, parent abandonment, etc. These occurrences have left their mark on you through programming, and they have prevented you from newer and greater opportunities in your life. You, and only you, can decide today to reprogram your way of thinking by challenging all your old ways.

Say the following words: "I am now aware that life in a way has programmed me in an unproductive way. As of today that old experiment on my life stops!" Rephrased differently, "My life is not a rat experiment! I will no longer flinch to the things that give me fear! I will not let those things that create fear in my mind control my life, my career, and my relationships."

Questions

1. Concerning education, is receiving a grade of "C" in a course a reason to withdraw? Is it rational to believe that you will always get an "A" in every subject? If getting a "C" or failing a class will not ultimately prevent you from reaching your goals, why would you consider withdrawing from the class? Do you now see how you have been programmed erroneously to believe that failing anything in life has little to do with what you will eventually accomplish?

2. Can you see rejection and failure as a positive? How? Can you name a moment in your life where being rejected or failing ended as a positive?

3. Do you understand that *every* successful person has been rejected or has failed much more than they succeeded? And others who have dropped out of the endeavor will never know if they would have been able to cross the finish line.

4. Looking back at your past, do you apply for the things you want in life, such as jobs, education, businesses, relationships, potential customers,

and others? Do you realize that not applying yourself to the things that you want in life is not rational? Do your now see that your biggest barriers are fear, ego, self-esteem, and overthinking?

5. Are you currently putting things on the back burner? Why do you think you are not taking the first step or the next step forward? Doesn't this automatically exclude you from succeeding, or is it that you feel safe from rejection? Understand, *learning to accept failure is a necessity to accomplishing success.*

Do not exclude yourself or let a third party reject or accept your efforts. Draft the résumé! Send it out! Wait for the rejection! No longer will you cater to your ego . . . it's your enemy and you should treat it as such. Distance yourself from your ego, your self-esteem, your fears, and your procrastination, because they have misled and betrayed you so far.

It's a new day; it's time to do things differently, time to get out of your comfort zone. It's time to confront the notions of failure, the notions of losing at something. It's time to wage the war against the fear of rejection.

Chapter 9

Does a little fish, swimming through the net's eye,
suffer from inferiority complex?

—Stanislaw Jerzy Lec

In October 1962, President John F. Kennedy, the second youngest president of the United States, was confronted with the possibility of nuclear war in the Cuban Missile Crisis. For 13 days, Cuba and Russia had nuclear missiles pointed at the US, and the US had nuclear weapons pointed at Cuba and Russia. It was a standoff with dire international consequences. When the press asked President Kennedy whether he had enough experience to handle this level of foreign affairs crisis, he responded (paraphrased), *No one is ready,* and this will be everyone's *first experience.* He made it a point to remind the inquisitors that every newly elected president has no presidential experience.

This stance by the president is codified in these slates of success that I share with you. The message to you is clear and concise: *Do not wait until you are qualified to apply.* Apply, learn, and work to become the most competent at your life's goals; this is your chance to create the most competent you. Taking any shortcuts in your goals will ultimately mean that you will not reach the apex of your career. Apply this message to the schools you wish to get in to, for the jobs that interest you, for any business that you wish to start, and for anything that requires a learning curve.

The saddest thing to observe in life is to witness humans walking, talking, and functioning as if they were casualties. Yes, you can go to any cemetery, anywhere in the world, and see tombstones of those who once lived, but to see people who are alive, but no longer living is a regretful shame. These are individuals who still walk and breathe, thus they can still fulfill their life's dreams or create newer, smaller ones. But they have resigned. They have given up. They have quit. The living dead, they are waiting for the caretaker to load them up on the gurney and transport them to the funeral parlor.

I wish I could whisper in their ears the following: "Lazarus, come forth! You are not dead; thus you can live, love, laugh, and have an impact on others. Why are you giving up when the journey is partially traveled?" The equivalent of a blood transfusion is needed for them, as many no longer know the purpose of their lives. It's time to readjust your glasses; it's time to take a better look at yourself; and it's time to question whether you really know the real you!

Vincent Van Gogh stated it this way, "If you hear a voice within you say 'you cannot paint,' then by all means paint, and that voice will be silenced."

Slate 3: Rebuilding Self-Perception

Everyone has hang-ups! That means that with life we now carry labels attached to us, as if they were scarlet letters. Labels that say, "You are lazy; you don't have a high-enough IQ; you are not that likeable; you don't have enough patience; you are not strong enough; you did not do well in school; and you are not as good as others. These are the biggest lies perpetrated on humans! Caste systems, debutante societies, sororities, fraternities, and these so-called clubs can never compare with the individual spirit that wishes to prevail.

Selling the idea that certain humans have more value than others is a gimmick by those who are currently in power. I have observed people in power—judges, members of Congress, athletes, businesspeople—act as if they were superior to others. I have seen people not in power accept that erroneous notion.

Today, you will no longer see a person in power in any superior fashion. To the contrary, you will work hard to challenge them and you will expose their weaknesses. It is the responsibility of schools, parents, and mentors early in life to explain this to the future generations. That positive self-perception can be taught and will enhance better learning. Looking at studies concerning teenagers gives us great indicators about self-perception forming early in life.

The National Association for Self Esteem has linked self-esteem to the following problems.

1. Poor grades
2. Teen pregnancy
3. Dropping out of school
4. Early sexuality
5. Bad acts, criminal acts
6. Alcohol and drugs
7. Overeating
8. Cheating

The key is either to prevent the younger generation from creating a destructive self-perception or reprogram the existing generation with a system of success. There are so many studies on how young boys and girls see themselves early in life. Sadly, according to dosomething.org, 70 percent of girls believe they don't measure up to society's standard. With the programming that is going on in today's hypervanity-based society, how could any young girl believe that she meets society's standards? And society condones the mental damage being perpetrated on these young teens.

It's time to strategically counteract this abuse done by the media and the so-called elites. Clearly, it's the teenage years where low-high self-esteem and lack of confidence is formed. If schools do not immediately tutor students on this essential subject, then seek a life coach. A life coach is skilled in scrubbing out the destructive paths of thinking in a young adult.

Sometimes the brain needs some housekeeping, a mental flossing, because over the years, erroneous concepts edge in. If this type of maintenance is not done regularly, then I would venture to say that one's thinking can get sidetracked. This would be a good period to hire a life coach, to speak to a mentor or anyone else who is trained to put you back on the track of productive thinking. Those without proper educational systems in place, or without access to the right mentoring, need to practice the slates of success until it becomes part of their muscle memory. The most coveted female in the 1960s, Marylyn Monroe, once publicly stated, "Wanting to be someone else is a waste of the person you are."

This note I discovered in Dante's twenty-pound bag of dog food.

> *Admiring others . . . but not seeing the beauty in yourself is the first order of business!*

If you develop low esteem, all the decisions that you make—marriage, college application, job search, or life decision—will be skewed against your favor. It's an anchor you can't afford.

Rid yourself of all these societal handcuffs and attack your dreams, like great boxer Muhammad Ali, like Indian entrepreneur Kalpana Saroj, like falsely imprisoned Jabbar Collins, like author Chris Gardner (*Pursuit of Happyness*), and like fashion designer Ralph Lauren . . . the list is long. These are individuals who embrace self and ignore society's negative input.

My daily polls on Facebook, BuzzFeed, and Twitter have resoundingly weighed in on the following question: "Tell us the reason that you did not reach your goals." I have tallied the results on this question with over 3,000 people of all ages, races, and gender. Here are the responses.

1. Self-esteem, shyness: 31 percent
2. Parents interfering: 19 percent
3. Lack of discipline, laziness: 13 percent
4. Fear, anxiety: 13 percent
5. Self-confidence: 11 percent
6. Bad decision-making: 9 percent
7. Self-abuse, addiction: 4 percent

It's like an epidemic! Such a large majority of individuals do not have the self-esteem and confidence to power forward and pursue their unique dreams. This should not be a reason why people do not pursue their dreams. **Sadly, this is the main reason why most people fail**. Do not let this be your reason.

Do not let your low self-esteem prevent you from challenging yourself publicly. You would think that if you don't compete publicly, and you don't experience defeat, that your ego would have less damage. This is a myth! *Your ego gets the most damaged when you do not compete, when you don't challenge yourself.* It could be joining a dance study, learning a new language, starting a new career, or entering a chess tournament. Over the years, you will look back and question yourself about why you didn't try. So, by all means, go at it and in the end you will feel better for losing versus never trying at all.

Make a list of your goals in column A: higher education, triple your sales, get more favorable verdicts, increase stores revenues, etc. Write in column B: Steps you will take that you have not done yet. In Column C: Make a list of *all the people who you will tell about these goals.* The caveat is to tell people when you are already working hard at it, not before you started it.

It has been discovered that if people verbalize their goals before they actually take real steps to accomplish them, those people will be less likely to reach the goals. Somehow, the brain accepts the verbalization has having accomplished the task; there is a satisfaction that relieves the person from actually completing the task. Avoid verbalizing your goals too early. Remember, this is not about making you feel better about yourself; this is about putting yourself in the best position to achieve what you want: losing weight, applying to college, or working longer hours. Thus, always wait until you have commenced your goals, taken concrete steps to achieve them, before you announce them publicly.

Questions

1. Look at the list of seven responses listed in this chapter. How many of those apply to you? Explain how one of these prevented you from forging ahead. If don't see a response that applies to you, think of one that does and answer the question.

2. Can you recall a particular event or experience in your life that lowered your self-esteem? For example, being left back in school; not being chosen on a team; or being rejected by family, friends, or community.

3. On any particular day, if you did two positive things and one negative thing, do you focus on the negative thing? Think about that, because most people don't realize how they focus on the negative. How about the people around you, would they talk more about the one negative thing you did or the two positive things you did?

4. Have you ever compared yourself to others and then felt worse about yourself? Where do you think you learned that habit?

5. Did teachers or guidance counselors inspire you to learn more, or did they make you lose interested in education?

"Good day, Norman, OK, I have nothing else for you today, I will see you tomorrow."

He put down his book and indicated to me that he had a job opportunity with the Sachem Central School District as an assistant wrestling coach. I smiled and voiced the following, "At least you will be with the ones who need you."

He looked puzzled by my statement but was too tired to engage with me at the moment. I turned my back and walked toward the bay windows, so that I could look out at the waves being produced by the Atlantic Ocean. As I repositioned myself to garner the view, I heard Norman walking down the stairs.

Chapter 10

*The chains of habit are too light to be felt
until they are too heavy to be broken.*

—Warren Buffett

I woke at 4:00 a.m., knowing that Norman had been appearing at the house about that time. I made my way down the stairs, carrying Dante like a potato sack, and prepared the morning coffee and steel-cut oatmeal. It was to my delight to look out the front door and not see Norman sitting on the stoop, so I took Dante for some fresh air. I saw Norman walking down Abner Drive. "Norman, why are you walking? You live over twenty miles from here!" He showed me his grease-covered hands and told me that his car had broken down. He was unable to repair it, so he walked the last three miles.

As I took him and Dante into the house, I told him that we would cover Slate 4 through Slate 6. He stated that he was more than ready, so I continued to speak.

I cannot over-state that creating good habits or eliminating bad habits is the most underestimated aspect of achieving success. It is underestimated, because small, bad habits sometimes become addictions, and many people who have addictions don't realize how the addiction started. Often it is by doing something that appears benign, something that doesn't appear to be a red flag. That's why so many potentially successful people end up on skid row. They never see it coming. There is a sense of arrogance and defiance that they are above habits and addiction. Prevention, avoidance is highly prudent and advised if you really wish to sustain wealth and success.

My friend, I must say that the strongest, the bravest, and the most talented have lost their battles to their heavy chains. The stories are unlimited about how so many humans have fallen to addictions, from the lowest to the highest. You would think that someone who has the knowledge and the dedication to graduate from an Ivy League school and built an empire would have what it takes to prevail over these lowly habits. Some of these individuals have dedicated over 20,000 hours to their careers, yet they couldn't find a fragment of that time to learn about prevention or neutralizing these bad habits. They have the wherewithal for the pursuit of perfection in their professions but not enough to prevent the chains that doom them.

Most people don't realize when the chains started to solidify. Fools believe that they can dabble with certain things in life: You can't just dine with her and then easily divorce yourself from her. Be warned that it would be much easier to become a millionaire, build an empire, get a doctoral degree, become a famous musician, or reach any of your other goals *than to detach yourself from her tentacles.*

Addiction's primary goal is for you to serve it faithfully; addiction's primary characteristic trait is jealousy, and it does want to share you with anyone—not your profession or your friends or your family. Addiction's greatest strength is that its initial appearance does not suggest danger; it will never wholly embrace you until you visit it religiously. It has been said that "Before you can break out of prison, you must realize you are locked up." And by the time that you see the prison cell, you have seriously handicapped yourself; you will be playing catch-up with the rest of society.

Pierre once left me this note in my boxing glove.

> *The person who is inferior to you without addictions will be your superior and will lavish in life while you beg.*

It is true that people with lesser talents and lesser commitments to their goals will often become champions over a more gifted person with an addiction. Over and over again, you will see the more talented person resign or drop out, and it will be the second or third place person who will receive the crown. For example, in reference to the Olympics, there have been over twenty-eight cases where gold medalists were stripped of first place, thus the second place was awarded the gold medal. There were over forty cases where the silver medalist was stripped of second place, and the third place was awarded the silver metal. And there were over fifty cases where a person did not place with a medal but was then awarded a bronze metal. Those statistics have been recorded since 1968.

There was once an Olympics where the 1st place winner was disqualified; thus the second place was awarded the Gold medal. Upon further review the number second, third, fourth and fifth were also disqualified by cheating in the competition. Compete, don't concern yourself if you are number six, five, four, three, or two in the competition, you actually might win the Gold.

The chains of bad habits and addictions are your enemy, especially when you take them casually. Avoid at all costs falling into the trap of bad habits that leads to addiction. Accomplishing your life desires are no match for getting caught up in an addiction. Becoming a millionaire is like graduating from elementary school compared to avoiding or overcoming a bad habit. You are forewarned! Whenever you see, smell, or touch a bad habit, put up a bold sign over it proclaiming, "NO FISHING!" Walk away.

Humans are creatures of habit. Never take it so lightly that what you do on a daily basis will not have an impact on your future. Every small, repetitive action practiced continuously will ultimately form into a giant—it will outgrow you. As we discussed in an earlier lesson, that's where you should use repetition for your benefit, not have repetition use you for its destruction.

Slate 4: Choosing Habits

So the next question is, "How do you replace your old methods and ways of living with a system that will put you on the right track?" That is the sequence that must occur. Let me submit to you an example of how to apply it in connection to bad habits. In 1960, Dr. Maxwell Maltz, a plastic surgeon, published a book that sold more than 30 million copies. *Psycho-Cybernetics* was based on how humans create and change their habits. After observing ninety-six patients, Maltz noticed that it took a minimum of twenty-one days to change any habit.

Some people have read his studies and have interpreted his studies to mean that you need twenty-one days to break a habit or create a habit. This is not completely accurate. What Maltz discovered was that a habit started to form on the twenty-first day, however, that didn't mean that it was solidified. As an example, if you were to stop smoking, on the twenty-first day you would either not have the compulsion to smoke or you would have a much lesser craving for it.

Maltz was running a medical facility that handled a lot of operations and medical experiments, including amputations. He once noticed after doing an amputation in his medical office that it took a patient twenty-one days after the surgery before a patient would start adjusting and addressing the new prosthetic. Because the leg was recently lost, the patient was not accustomed to the void of the leg. Prior to the twenty-one days, the patient acted as if the leg was still whole. It was at the twenty-one day mark that the doctor started noticing the patient making adjustments.

Any habit that you can think about will become part of you with repetition. It could be as simple as putting your car keys on a kitchen table versus your bedroom nightstand, double locking your door at night, or smoking a cigar. Twenty-one days is the beginning threshold of any habit forming or any habit breaking.

Today is the first day that we have addressed the issues that have destroyed the most talented people in history. The most destructive forces facing humankind are the habits that we keep and allow in ourselves. Consider, contemplate, or write down the bad habits in your life that have prevented you or will prevent you from being successful.

Also, on a lighter note, there are personality habits that most people ignore but can also derail your success. For example, oversensitivity when being judged, rejecting positive changes, wanting to quit when you are losing, thinking that others are smarter, relying on what others think about you, feeling entitled, lack of motivation, making bad choices in your life, constantly noticing your weaknesses, following the crowd, etc.

As philosopher Will Durant stated, "We are what we repeatedly do." As simple as this sounds, you need to reprogram your thoughts. The world you live in has held the remote control of your life, including your habits. In life, there are things such as being lazy that obviously will destroy your chances of becoming successful, and then there are things that are subtler but just as damaging to your success. Do not become a casualty to the subtle.

Achieving your goals is so much more gratifying that anything you can give up. Change is near. Develop the ability to find a weakness, write it down, and fight it for twenty-one days to begin the removal process. If you can't detect a flaw or a bad habit in yourself, feel free to ask someone who knows you, and my guess is that you will get an earful. Yes, I should add something else to that equation to make it complete. I learned it from the first puzzle piece that Pierre gave me.

> *It is easier to prevent bad habits*
> *than to break them.*
> —Benjamin Franklin

You should now see after this lesson, how we are in control of making or breaking a habit. There is a system built into humans that Dr. Maltz noted in his bestselling book. If we don't take action for a certain time period, the habits just get more ingrained in our way of living and acting. Programming our minds through a mundane repetition of certain actions is a crucial step to becoming more productive and reversing the past ingrained training.

Let not the winds of life drift you in the wrong directions. This slate on habit is like the thief in the night—it creeps into people's lives when they least expect. Most people have two or three decades of habits that have been formed. Even if you have been trained by the military, a rigorous academic education, or have a strong religious background, there are habits that have been formed. Don't confuse all your accomplishments with the idea that all humans formulated habits, intentionally or unintentionally. Bad habits are not your best friend; they are not you; they don't add anything positive to your life; they wreck your life. Spotting them early is the first step to overcoming them. And, of course, the second step is to understand that breaking out of an addiction is nearly impossible without professional help, *which is why avoiding addictions is best.*

I can tell you that I have spoken to over 4,000 people who had addictions and invariably there are six that always raise their ugly heads.

1. drug addiction
2. food addiction
3. sexual addiction
4. nicotine addiction
5. alcohol addiction
6. gambling addiction

Get a blank piece of paper. Write down your bad habits. If you write fewer than six of them, you need to rethink this issue, or ask people close to you and I bet the list will double. You do realize that a bad habit could mean excessive use of the internet, watching too much television, shopping for items you don't need, unwarranted anger, etc.

I noticed something troubling after interviewing over 350 people about their bad habits. There was a pattern and a consensus of certain bad habits that everyone was aware of, but there was also something I colloquially named the "blind spots"! Everyone, without exception missed certain habits that were capable of derailing their future success. I realized it after giving them a series of over fifty scenarios and noticing their shortcomings. In addition, the closest person to them was just a phone call, a text, or an email away, and it was lucrative for me to utilize them. These blind-spot habits are more dangerous to them than those that have been brought to their attention for years.

Allow me to give you an example of one of them. Consider a person who has a "lack of structure" in his or her life. You rarely hear about people blaming another person's failures due to that issue. It's much easier, much safer, to say that the person lacked discipline, but be on notice that there are habits that are not as translucent, not as easy to identify.

Sticking with the issue of lack of structure, this is a flaw that usually develops early in life. For example, a child is allowed to not follow any house rules, including, but not limited to, unlimited hours of watching television, playing video games, listening to music, and interacting with friends. If the structure is not built early in life, or it is not reversed as an adult, then that individual will fall prey to many other interests in life that will take away from their achievements in the future. There is a long list of these blind spots that escape the average person's assessment. A mentor, a prepared parent, or a life coach can address these on an individual basis.

Just so you don't feel bad, Benjamin Franklin wrote a book on the thirteen virtues he felt that he needed to improve on. He took one virtue and worked on that virtue for seven days. Some of the things he felt he needed to improve on were temper, hard work, sincerity, and humility. He was twenty years old at the time.

Your net worth to the world is usually determined by what remains after your bad habits are subtracted from your good ones.
—Benjamin Franklin

Questions

1. What are your obvious bad habits that you must get rid of? Pick one: for example. waking up late, consuming too much sugar, spending too many hours on the internet, smoking, swearing, purchasing unnecessary items, etc.

2. Which bad habit would you like to work on first? Try this experiment. As of today, pick one of your bad habits and avoid it for ten days. Do not pick the most difficult bad habit that you have, as it's best to start with the one that you think does not have any tentacles on your life. If you fail and engage in the bad habit within the ten days,

let it go and pick another bad habit and try to avoid it for ten days. This experiment will reveal to you who is currently in charge of your life, you or your habit. This will also show you how vulnerable you might be to future worse habits. *Your skill, your talent, and your intelligence will not save you from a habit you cannot break.*

3. What is a blind-spot bad habit that you need to work on?

4. Do you recognize that some of your current bad habits have been carried over from your past? What are two of them? For example, bad temper, lashing out, being inconsiderate to others, laziness, or quitting things prematurely. These should concern you.

5. Are there things that you are currently doing daily—like eating dessert late at night, drinking alcohol more frequently, or cursing—that you didn't do last year? Name them. Spot them out. Call them out.

6. Who has mentored you for the struggles of life and career?

Chapter 11

*And let us not be weary in well doing: for in due
season we shall reap, if we faint not.*

—Galatians 6:9, KJV

For those who have ears, let them hear. There
is a point in any battle, any endeavor, and any
real challenge when your will, your mind, wishes
to wave the white flag. Champions and non-champions experience this point. It is an inevitable wall.
All of us have to confront this point, if we wish to
find the strongest person within us. This is the point
where your natural conscious has nothing else to
give, however, your subconscious, your inner self,
has to take over.

Some people call this a second wind, and other
people call this being in the zone. You will never
hit the "zone" or your "second wind" if you stop at
this wall. The wall is a part of every challenge—be
it a closing argument in a trial, a wrestling match, or
creating the lyrics to a song—where the natural self

wants to stop or is stumped. Artist, musicians, and writers, not just people who compete for a living, know about this place.

Once you reach this point, you should know that the ending, victory is near. This critical stage, when your natural thoughts are contemplating resigning, doesn't last long, it's just the most painful. But you can't let the physical or mental pain, lack of creativity, or exhaustion take over. You must stop thinking about the physical or the "the flesh." The way to do this is to stop thinking about the endeavor and keep moving forward. When you do that, you will enter a different realm that doesn't feel like pain, exhaustion, or physical. Here is where all great endeavors have been achieved, *after you hit the wall, not before.* Remember that and you will know the *sequence of success.*

Slate 5: Passing the Wall

At this stage, you are only three slates away from knowing this belief system of success. You are not going to "ring the bell" until you have proven to yourself that you are open and willing to adhere to a new set of principles that were not taught to you in your previous years. Most likely, you are working hard to understand these principles, because you have not had a mentor, a life coach, or a person who trained you for success in your career and achievements! You are a survivor, you are willing and able to adapt to your past failures or your status quo life to reach your goals. This might sound like an overstatement, but for some individuals these principles might save their life, thus, so it's worth all the effort in the world.

Most humans learn early in life whether they are advancing forward or moving backward in their lives. Ignoring academic, mental, or physical failures when you're young is common place; however, as we get closer to graduating from high school, it becomes apparent that we are not succeeding, that we are letting ourselves down, and that others have also let us down. It's a sobering realization. But life does not have any do-overs! Now, you must trust in these lessons and these age-old theories that were given to me by individuals who lived thousands of years ago.

Working hard is not a natural instinct for humans. To the contrary, I have learned that human instinct is to do the least possible work and wish for the greatest harvest. Humans' natural instinct is not to work hard. Acknowledge it in yourself and in others. *Never believe that successful people don't feel lazy . . . everyone has that trait.* It might just be the way our brains are programmed to conserve energy for fight or flight.

Hard work is not a here or there, maybe today or maybe tomorrow. Hard work is a consistent dedication to our chosen friend. So the most successful don't operate on the flight-or-fight mode; they operate on fighting each round, one at a time, until their mission has been accomplished. Thus the most successful wake up every morning to perform their tasks without distinction. They leave emotions out of it. It's not a do-or-die decision. It's an action of do.

You have come too far to turn back! Only a small fraction of society would have been at this point in the lessons. This is the breaking point, this is where you leave your competition behind or fall back to the point in your life where you left off prior to reading these slates. The difference between a winner and a loser is but a fraction of a second! However, to the person who loses, it feels beyond his or her grasp.

Remember this, *that you have always been so close to getting the lifestyle that was meant for you, you never realized that turning that last corner would have revealed your destination.* Be it becoming a Navy SEAL, running a marathon, getting your doctorate, closing more sales than the top agent, or becoming certified in your life profession . . . .it's all nearby, nothing is that far away, nothing!

> *That is the secret that nobody wants you to know.*

Don't believe me. Watch when Muhammad Ali fought Joe Frazier in the third fight. Look at Ali *before* Frazier's corner threw in the towel. What did you see? Ali was done, defeated, dead, exhausted, and had nothing left! So it's time to put this principle into practice, that whatever you do in your life . . . . shortcuts always turn out to be long cuts. If you go to the gym, and you usually do ten repetitions, are those repetitions only with 80 percent effort? If they are, only do eight repetitions, but give them 100 percent. If you work an eight-hour shirt, make sure that you did not only do five hours of work. If your school report calls for ten pages, do not submit six pages of good content and four pages of filler. Sometimes it might appear that you are doing less, but in reality you are not taking any shortcuts.

Questions

1. In any competition, at what stage do you hit the wall: beginning, middle, or end? Is the "wall" similar to what is referred to as a "second wind"?

2. When you enter the zone called the "second wind," do you feel more struggle/more pain or less struggle/less pain?

3. An assignment has a timeline to finish in seven days. Would you prefer to have an employee who crams and pushes the assignment and finishes in three days, or would you prefer to have an employee who evenly spreads work out and finishes in five days? Why?

So, life can be long . . . according to Nadira, and I agree with her! The next twenty-one days always do more than is requested of you. Never just do what is required of you, without fail, always submit more. Unless you can invent a system that gets you more productive doing less work. Your options are to *create methods that are more productive for your activities or put more work into it* . Do not allow others or the world to dictate your work product. This is often called going the extra mile.

If your goals require an extra two miles, then deliver it without reservation. It is as simple as it sounds. Believe me, your competitors are not following these principles. And if you run into someone who is, count your blessings, because you will learn a lot about yourself if you are forced into these late rounds.

I share another of Pierre's notes.

Endurance is the sibling of victory and heroism, you can't have one without the other.

Chapter 12

A man sat by a fireplace and yelled, "Give me heat!"
The fireplace responded, "Give me wood."

—Author Unknown

Slate 6: Work as If You Were Overpaid

Whether it is a school grade, getting a new job, or getting involved in a new relationship, people often have preconceived notions of their value. Maybe your credentials, your diplomas, and your experience are highly desired, however, if you wish to be successful, you have to put that aside and deliver first and deliver more than what you are paid for. This is the secret that seems to have confounded many employees. They are asking for heat when the company is requiring productivity! Now don't get me wrong, you can probably keep a job in this competitive world, but to advance, to gain bonuses, and to surpass the peloton, *one needs to give more than one receives.*

I have seen relationships where each person is just doing their half. If you only give half, and the other person only gives half, then what is the most you will receive? The answer is 50 percent. On the other hand, if you do more for your partner, without expecting them to equal your efforts, then one of two things will happen: one, he or she will open up to do more for you; and two, he or she will be selfish and you will know that it is not reciprocated. The same applies in business.

Pierre's note enlightened me on this distinction.

> *Selflessness versus selfishness. Guess who wins?*

On many occasions, people have told me that they have given 110 percent to their goals, and it resulted in them becoming "burned out." At other times, people have told me that they couldn't get motivated on that level due to a spectrum of reasons. Here is where one needs to understand the theory of "flow." In 1975, psychologist Mihaly Csikszentmihalyi was given credit for labeling the term flow. It is a mental state, a state of mind, in which a person is functioning at his or her *most productive level without necessarily working harder.*

In this state of flow, time, environment, and location becomes secondary to the task being performed. The person performing the task is immersed, without thought or much deliberation. A person in this mental state can outperform an individual working harder than he or she is. It is argued that humans are happiest in this state of mind, as opposed to the other seven states of minds that are experienced in learning and dealing with challenges. The other state of minds are anxiety, apathy, arousal, boredom, control, relaxation, and worry.

In the flow state of mind, everything is easier without stress, anxiety, or deliberations. If, for example, you don't feel challenged at your school or at work, it might be that you are in one of the other seven states of mind. It applies to sports, music, business, school, art, and other activities. There is a more detailed definition of flow in positive psychology books and periodicals, however, for our purposes ,this definition will suffice. I should mention that when you are not operating in the flow state of mind, then your success and your happiness decreases.

This concept of flow was coined in 1975, however, similar to the theory of visualization, it was given to me by Pierre's books and writings dating back thousands of years ago. In one of the books left by Pierre about Taoism, the theory of flow was described as "oneness of self" and "being at one with things." That is, when a person is physically working on a task, mentally they become married to that task, as if they were one!

An example that will take flow out of theory and into real life was given by Ayrton Senna, the greatest Formula One driver of all time, when he said,

> Suddenly I was nearly two seconds faster than anybody else, including my team mate with the same car. And suddenly I realised that I was no longer driving the car consciously. I was driving it by a kind of instinct, only I was in a different dimension. It was like I was in a tunnel. Not only the tunnel under the hotel, but the whole circuit was a tunnel. I was just going and going, more and more and more and more. I was way over the limit, but still able to find even more.

When you enter the state of flow, you surpass any human experience.

Let's look at your past experiences. Pick any three subjects in your life. For example, schools, jobs, and friendships. Starting tomorrow, concentrate on doing extra work on one of those endeavors. All you need is one time of the week to do more than you would have done in the past. You will notice in a short time not only how you are advancing in that endeavor but you will also notice how others will start to recognize the extra effort put out by you. In school, your grades will improve if you give your studies an extra thirty minutes. At the job, your supervisor will notice you and, in turn, you'll have job stability and a reputation for going the extra mile. In a friendship, your friend will appreciate you more and will be more apt to return the kindness.

Questions

1. When is last time you appeared at work early? Do you realize that at work everyone notices everything you do, although they do not acknowledge it?

2. When you hand in a project, do you just meet the minimum requirements?

3. When you pay your bills, do you submit them early?

4. Starting today, throughout your day, remind yourself that you are overpaid in life. If you don't believe that, just visit any cemetery or look through the obituaries and ask yourself if any one of those people would hesitate for a second to switch places with you?

Let's be honest with ourselves. When we are obsessed, when we desire, when we are driven by what we want, we shut everything out. This type of concentration on our goals must be sustained until we attain the desired results, especially during certain stages. For example, studying for the bar examination to be admitted as an attorney. If during the six or so weeks that you are preparing, you find yourself diverted to other responsibilities, then your likelihood of success is greatly diminished.

Some of our goals can be accomplished in weeks and others can take years. Thus, it is up to you, so you must determine when to peak and when to stay in the state of flow. If you ever feel that you don't have that feverish desire for your career, your relationship, or your hobby, then you can either continue it, knowing that you will not hit the height of it, or you can withdraw from it and find something else that you desire. I know it sounds extreme, however, life is to be lived with desire, not with complacency. *Complacency is the enemy, it's the undertaker before the funeral.* Wake up, have desire for your dreams, and conquer your life's dreams.

It was Michael Jordan who confidently stated, "My body could stand the crutches but my mind couldn't stand the sidelines." In other words, his obsession to compete could not be broken, even though his bones could. Whether consciously or subconsciously, he entered his zone. Zone is a place that only knows one thing . . . *fight, not flight.* It's a mental state that requires no thought, no premeditation, no fear, and no concern for anything other than grasping the goal.

I have seen fighters with broken arms, broken jaws, broken ribs, who box their way to victory. I have witnessed soldiers with bullets throughout their bodies attack the enemy. I have seen people who die to protect their children from danger. It's a place that transcends the natural, because nothing else matters when you enter it, as all your human limitations are left behind.

Get there! No matter how, get there. If you do not strive in competition for this destination, then you are limited in your capacity to win. I don't care about your IQ. I don't care about your strengths. I don't care about your reputation. You will be overtaken by the person who competes in this mental state. Please understand that achievement is about desire. If you have no real desire, you will have no real victory.

◼

"Good night, Norman, and, yes, this lesson went overtime. Always remember this proverb, "And let us not be weary in well doing: for in due season we shall reap, if we faint not" (Galatians 6:9, KJV). I have lived a long life, and I have never fainted!"

Chapter 13

Slate 7: Visualization

By day number three, Norman was sitting in the attic with Dante, waiting for me to climb up the stairs and finalize the seventh slate of success.

I petted the human, who was pretending to be a dog, and touched Norman on his shoulder, like a father would do when he is showing pride to his son on a rare occasion. I stood over both of them and spoke.

One of the greatest tools that so many successful individuals have used to gain the proper mindset is called *visualization*. I will not get too deep into the science behind the concept of visualization, however, I will describe how I used visualization to do closing arguments in various criminal jury trials, in full contact, kick-boxing matches, writing books, and flying single-engine airplanes.

For the purposes of this book, visualization slightly differs from meditation in that *visualization* is focused on a particular problem, while *meditation* is a form of controlling and relaxing yourself. That is, visualization is used for problem solving, while meditation is used for relaxing. Meditation has also been utilized since antiquity for achieving success. It was used by the Taoist in China and the Buddhist in India. The reason I quickly mention meditation is that visualization originates from it. However, to achieve the principles of success, you do not need to study meditation. It is enough to know that meditation is the grandfather of visualization.

All over the world, visualization has been used for losing weight, running marathons, struggling with cancer, passing an exam, performing at a trial, writing songs, etc. Aymeric Guillot, PhD, a professor in France at the Center of Research and Innovation concluded that *real-world and imaginary thoughts are similar*. This conclusion was based on scientific research.

Suffice to say, if you go into a real competition, or you imagine going into that competition, the mind senses it as the same. This is important to realize, because if one imagines an event over and over again, prior to the event, then in a way one has practiced that event before the actual appearance. I have done it hundreds of time in my profession as a trial lawyer. I would be unprepared in any of my trials if I did not imagine the location, the circumstances, the voices, the people in that courtroom, and my general arguments to the jury.

Visualization and meditation are similar in one manner, that is, they both require for you to be alone in a quiet place without distractions. Prior to every jury trial, prior to any competition, I would sit in a semi-dark room for a least one hour. I would think about the most damaging facts against my client and just let my subconscious ponder those. Then I would be in a state of relaxation, a nonfocused state of mind, to allow my mind to flow with possible solutions.

To be specific, I would start imagining the walls of the courtroom, the judge who would preside, and how the jury members would stare at me blankly. I would then imagine myself speaking the case to the jury over and over again. Sometimes nothing would be conjured up quickly, and sometimes my mind would flow with many rebuttals.

I have never practiced in this resting state of mind without a solution! However, I have attempted to resolve problems with my subconscious and focused my mind without any results. I would repeat this process for two or three sessions until my creative mind had no additional input. In this process, without trying, without writing, and without any intent, ideas start to appear and I start to visualize the trial before me. This is because I have no distractions, just me and the information in my mind. *Visualization can even occur in one's sleep, however, the experts have yet to write about this phenomenon!* I discovered that there comes a point in those sessions when I realized that I was ready to perform.

Recently, I spoke to one of the most sought-after life coaches on the East Coast, who is also the coauthor of a book about visualization techniques—Dawn Nic. After her bestselling book, *Success Mastery*, was released, I asked her why visualization was so successful with athletes. Her response was as follows.

> The beauty of visualization is that it uses all of the five senses. The mental imagery allows our sympathetic nervous system to respond in a way that helps us to resolve conflict, to control our breathing patterns, which

regulates the heart rate . . . it even goes as far as helping our bodies heal. The mind is our most powerful tool, so use it to do good onto others and ourselves.

Visualization is not just for athletes, although they have been the ones who have gained the most benefit from this age-old principle. This book is not long enough to mention the famous people who have used this technique to accomplish their goals. Do the research on visualization and you will be astounded on how it is supported by the science and sports community.

Jerry Figgiani, an eighth dan black belt in Shorin Ryu Karatedo International, in his book written with Chris R. Vaccaro called *The Difference: A Mental Approach to Martial Arts,* discusses how he trains his students under hostile situations to confront and conquer life-and-death environments with the methods of visualization. As one of the renowned martial artists in the country, Sensei Figgiani understands the undeniable power of using the mind to practice techniques before they are physically executed. In other words, he is teaching that the movements, the techniques, and the persons surroundings should exist in the mind and in the physical.

I will end this session with a statement from an iconic inventor, Nikola Tesla,

> My method is different. I do not rush into actual work. When I get a new idea, I start at once building it up in my imagination, and make improvements and operate the device in my mind. When I have gone so far as to embody everything in my invention, every possible improvement I can think of, and when I see no fault anywhere, I put into concrete form the final product of my brain.

Why isn't visualization mainstream? Noticed that Tesla believed (in the 1890s) that his method of invention "is different" due to his visualization techniques. Yet visualization was spoken about by the great Roman orator, politician, and lawyer Cicero in 63 BCE. Cicero, in his discussions, would reference visualization as the "mentis oculi." Many great leaders, like Tesla, believe that they discovered the method of visualization, but these methods have been captured thousands of years ago. This is why the principles of success given to me by Pierre have to be passed down systematically to the younger generations.

Science often confirms what great philosophers, clergy, and coaches of life have known for thousands of years. In 2001, neurologist Marcus E. Raichle from the Washington University School of Medicine coined the term "default mode." Without getting too deep with neuroscience, default mode is where a brain continues to operate, even at a rest mode, that is, it does not deactivate just because an individual stops "thinking." Ideas, strategies, concepts, and creativity are still flowing in the same part of the brain.

Many people believe erroneously that to resolve a problem, to create a solution, one has to focus on the problem to find a solution. Science now shows that the energy in the brain is working at a similar level when one stops focusing and one relaxes, settles back, and enters a resting state. Sounds exactly like slate 7, *which has assisted me in creating winning arguments before trial juries for over twenty years.* It's a conscious state, but it is a state of mind where the individual is no longer concentrating, no longer focusing on the problems at hand, but sitting back and allowing the imagination, the subconscious, the *default mode* to work out the solutions.

I recommend a way to write down or record the solutions that one gets from these sessions. Is this how the great composer Wolfgang Amadeus Mozart composed entire symphonies without writing a single note on paper? Was he using the default mode of his brain to capture creativity beyond other composers, who just sat, practiced, and focused?

In 1929, the inventor of the electroencephalogram proposed the idea that the brain is always active. At that time, the science community rejected the notion. The scans taken of the brain during certain types of meditation prove that structural changes in the default mode of the brain are activated. Many in the science community are now claiming that the brain becomes more creative during this default mode! This is partially due to the lack of interruption in everyday tasks and the lack of overconcentration. So, find that place where you can rest and awaken that inner part of your brain.

Let me be as clear as day for you on this lesson. Singlemindedness, also known as focus, sometimes referred to as an obsession, is a prerequisite for complete success. Too many individuals are balancing many goals and projects on their plates, the one who prevails is the one with a clear game plan for life. As the great educator and author Peter Drucker once said, "The single-minded ones, the monomaniacs, are the only true achievers."

A great Greek philosopher was once asked by his student what was focus and how could someone be so focused to achieve their goals? The teacher took the student to the ocean and attempted to drown the student, where the student was losing the fight and gasping for his life. Then he asked the bewildered student this question, "How many things were you thinking about when your head was under the water? How many of your problems did you ponder?" With absolute confidence, the philosopher answered his own question. "None. You had only one thing on your mind and that was not to drown."

My friend once wrote me something similar.

> It's in the dark places; it's in the painful places; it's in the lonely places that the mind sees the light.

Starting today, you will focus on one task at a time. There is no such thing as multitasking where you are jumping from one thing to the other. Each thing that you do still needs to be done perfectly, and that requires your total attention.

In the mornings, or before you go to sleep, make a short list of the things that you believe are your priorities for that day. This should take no more than ten minutes. After twenty-one days of making these lists, you can continue the list making, or you can do this exercise mentally.

If you have ever been to a child's sporting event, take a look at some of their eyes as they are competing to score. You will notice an intense desire that you should still have in your life. If you don't, you are missing that edge in your life that is necessary to prevail. The opposite of watching children compete is taking a walk through a cemetery. At that location, there is no longer any effort, motivation, or life.

Look around from now on and seek that look in people's eyes. It will remind you what you should never allow yourself to lose. You might be able to find this look in some of your old photos. See yourself at a different time and how you had a different set of eyes, ones that were hungry to learn, to love, and to live. I cannot overstate how you need to acknowledge this look. Find five people, around you or in photos, and see that aspiration in their eyes.

Questions

1. Find a photo of your childhood. Look hard at it. Have you lost any positive character trait since that time period? Can you see the person in that

photo as having a clean slate? Can you try to clean up all the negative things that you have been carrying since those years?

2. Have you ever thought of a really good idea or a solution in a state of just sitting, relaxing, or resting?

3. Do you find yourself trying to solve a problem or tap into your creativity, but just draw a blank due to intense focusing?

Chapter 14

The Mindsets

Without the proper mindset, sustaining success for long periods of time can become futile. Think of it like this. Imagine someone goes on an impractical diet that allows them to lose many pounds in the beginning phases, however, in the latter stages the weight ultimately gets reacquired. Or imagine a person who operates a business and becomes profitable by way of a compromised product. Attaining success because you have the skills, work ethics, and prosperity doesn't assure that you will keep it long term.

Having said that, these are the seven *mindsets* that I gathered from 500 people who captured and sustained success throughout their lives, I use a twenty-five-year standard. It's not likely that after twenty-five years, they would surrender the belief system that they adopted and lived with. As a private attorney for twenty-five years, I have personally interviewed 126 of these successful people. They varied in professions, from athletes to real estate developers. Of course, there were many wealthy doctors, lawyers, and sales executives.

There were 200 who shared their belief systems on the issue of long-term sustainability. I researched anything they had been written or recorded, including biographies, blogs, and their profiles from the beginning of their careers. In addition to the 126 interviews, 174 answered my poll questions that I asked on all the major social media sites. Yes, I ask a lot of questions, including follow-up questions based on their initial responses.

The mindset necessary to apply the above belief system contains the following seven attributes.

1. Conquer insatiability. Often we think of the things that we don't have and *not of the things we do have.* So our minds are always looking for something far and away and not saluting our current status. You need to change this mindset to be able to appreciate your career and your accomplishments. This mindset does not contradict the mindset that creates goals and future visions in life. This is more about "the now."

Appreciate the accomplishments that you have made and *visualize how you would feel if you lost the things that you currently possess.* An example of practicing negative visualization would be the following. Imagine working in your current status, in school or at work as a homeless person. This is not farfetched. Take the movie that Will Smith starred in called *The Pursuit of Happyness.* It's the true story of a father who lived in a homeless shelter, as he pursued his dreams of working and succeeding at a prestigious brokerage firm. This mindset was practiced and adopted by Socrates, Seneca, Epictetus, Marcus Aurelius, and others in the early third century BCE. The Greeks and Romans called it stoicism. In today's society, humans live their lives being insatiable, chasing their tails never to catch them.

2. Reject "genius effect." When we see someone who we perceive as excelling in school, at work, or at an event, and look at them as if their accomplishments required something mystical or genius . . . it's a strange phenomenon. As long as you see a winner as some superhero, then you can justify in your mind why you can't accomplish the exact thing or surpass it. If you have ever watched horses at racetracks, you will notice that they wear "blinders" so that they do not notice the sprinter to the left or right. The blinders are for the purpose of preventing distractions to the horse in the race. So, on your journey to career success, never take off your blinders, just run your race.

3. Adaptation. To quote Charles Darwin, "It is not the strongest of the species that survives, nor the most intelligent that survives. It is the one that is most adaptable to change." Of the answers that I received from the 500 successful people who I write about, all of them gave this as an answer for long-term success and sustainability: *adaptability and flexibility*. Although it is not the most dynamic of mindsets, it is the most necessary in having long-term success.

Most people see adaptation in a linear fashion, like adjusting to a new manager, new policies, or a new job. Adaptation is necessary and most important when we are succeeding. I am reminded of Steve Jobs, the cofounder of Apple, when he was first terminated from Apple at the age of thirty. When he returned to Apple, over a decade later, he had conquered his weaknesses along with his people and leadership skills.

4. Manage expectations. It is so easy to convince yourself that your path to success is not going according to schedule. When in reality, there will be advances, stalemates, and digression in all journeys. Thus, we cannot look at any one period of time and broad brush it with your entire pursuit. Accept and embrace the failures and the periods of digression; they are all part of the course.

Remind yourself of the principles of insatiability and the genius effect from time to time, because they are interwoven with managing your expectations. Think about it. Expectations are just ideas in your head, a desire to receive something. Don't ever let these ideas derail your real path to success. The work you do, the study that you do, the principles you live by are the real workhorses in your success, not your expectations. As the expression goes, "Expectations are premeditated resentments." *Create a mindset that is based on actions, not desirable ideas.*

"Norman, we ran late today and there are only three mindsets left that we need to discuss to complete all the lessons, so why don't we finish in the morning?"

With dark circles under his eyes, it was obvious that he was in agreement. Norman appeared to be concerned, and I didn't understand why until he spoke. "What happens after the final lesson tomorrow? Can I still come over to share tea with Nadira?"

I paused, and I realized then that he needed her, as a child needs a mother. I placed my hand around his shoulder and told him that neither Nadira or I would abandon him. It struck me after looking at my watch that Nadira had not eaten yet.

I love that Nadira's favorite dish is pasteles— vegetables, pork, or beef wrapped with brown rice and covered in a green banana leaf during the cooking process. She loves all Colombian food. For her, I have always paired that dish with a mango lassi beverage. This particular Friday evening, about 8:00 p.m. after she was finished with dinner, she asked me if I could read to her. She would always tear up in the beginning of *The Count of Monte Cristo* when Fernand, the antagonist character in the book, betrayed Edmond Dantès unjustifiably by having him arrested at his own wedding . . . at the height of his happiness.

Edmond was young, loving, hardworking and naïve to the wickedness of the world. But just like the biblical betrayal of Jesus at the hands of Judas

Iscariot, Fernand met a similar fate . . . suicide. As I read her that tragic chapter, Nadira continued to cry. I timed the closing of the book before her eyelids joined. I whispered to her, knowing that she could hear me, because her eyes had that muscle contraction that only exists in the first stage of sleep, "Don't be weary, you know that Edmond has no quit in him!" She smiled with her eyes shut. I always protected her from harm.

At about 10:00 p.m. after I was done answering about two hours of questions on my blog, I went back to Nadira and kissed her good night. As my lips blindly touched hers, she instinctively said in her nightdream, "I love bourbon!" Without hesitation, I responded, "I know dollface! You used to drink more of it than me!" In my wonder, I asked her, "Did you just lick my lips?" She smiled sheepishly.

It's amazing to me that people deprive themselves of some of the finest pleasure because of the stigma attached to them by society, by religion, and by community norms. Not Nadira, she lavished in the delights of life without hesitation or remorse. She taught me how to unburden myself by shedding my religious straitjacket. Often she would say to me, "You do realize that we are alone, nobody is watching or judging you!"

She was right, however, when you are programmed at an early age in life, particularly through strict parents and Catholic schools, it is difficult to ignore that voice from within. That voice that was drilled into your head from youth, that voice that constantly repeated the same old mantra: "Every day you will be in sin, and every day you will be repenting." It's a hard lesson to overcome, especially when you were raised under such a strict upbringing, were disciplined by nuns, and attended radical churches as a young adult. It was social reformer Susan B. Anthony who was quoted as stating, "I distrust those people who know so well what God wants them to do, because I notice it always coincides with their own desires."

Chapter 15

*When educating the minds of our youth, we must
not forget to educate their hearts.*

—Dalai Lama

As I woke the next day at 4:00 a.m., there was
that distinct aromatic smell of Colombian
coffee. Walking down the stairs, I noticed Norman
sitting in my kitchen.

"Good morning, sir!" he said unabashed.

"I won't even ask how you got in," I responded.
"I see that you're ready for the final three lessons."

He appeared to be different, even his dress
attire was polished and coordinated, as opposed
to the first day I met him. I remembered the look
that Norman sported; it was the look of someone
young who was about to make a conquest in this
world. Norman had that look; it was in his eyes,
in his walk, and especially in his voice. I finally
realized that he looked as I once looked about three
decades ago, when I was unaccomplished but was

ready to have an impact on the brothers and sisters of this world. Nothing like knowing that you have worked so hard, have committed so much effort in accomplishing the unattainable, and now it is the attainable! Norman and I have rounded the bases together, so now I know that there is a beginning and an end to all human life, all accomplishments.

5. Toughmindedness. Nothing in life will come easy. There is no easy road. If there is no struggle, there is no progress. We have all heard these sayings. Now you need to add this mindset to your personality, for without it, you will stopped at every turn. Your weaknesses, we all have weaknesses, will be called out by your professors, your supervisors, and even your loved ones. The opposite of toughmindedness is being sensitive or overly sensitive. A toughminded person will take a criticism and not personalize it, and then improve and remedy that weakness. A sensitive person will believe that every criticism is an attack. Moreover, if a person is sensitive and feels entitled by a personality trait, then no progress will ever be made.

6. Fuel the vision. Please do not drop your guard on this mindset. I don't mean a Gandhi, Jesus,

Moses, or Mother Teresa vision. I am telling you that you have to program your mind to see things, experience *things that will generate enthusiasm in your pursuit of success.* How often have we taken a taxi ride, and we see a photo of the driver's family, child, or mother? *Often* is the answer. Why? Because the hours are rough, the pay is low, the customers are not respectful, and it is dangerous. The photo is the fuel that will get that taxi driver to his/her destination in life. I am a true believer in writing your goals on paper or an index card and keeping the paper in your pocket. So, when you reach to grab your money, your keys, or any object, you will be fueled by touching the paper with your aspirations on it. Again, please do not take this mindset lightly, because it is easy to *take our eyes off the ball,* as one of the millionaires I spoke to kept reminding me.

7. Action vs. perfectionism. Perfectionism is a form of procrastination. Perfectionism is a safety net, a safe space. Stop avoiding judgment! Stop avoiding failure! It's only when you take the next step that you can learn, improve, and rectify your weaknesses. Shatter that ego for the sake of advancement and progression.

"Norman, you have completed all the materials that were passed down to me. These include Pierre's box, combined with all of the adaptions made by me after twenty-five years of running a successful law practice, surviving near-death crashes in my Cessna, and competing in various competitions, including fighting, dancing, and bodybuilding."

He stood there, silently waiting for further instructions; he knew my way of thinking. He asked me point blank, "Do you think Pierre would have approve that you modified the materials given to you in that box?"

I smiled and replied, "He expected me to update those materials to address the problems that apply to today's youth and modern society."

I continued. "Let me explain something to you, Norman. Pierre included hundreds of pages of notes. Those notes were in his handwriting. Pierre must have adapted the works of our previous inspirational writers and orators. That means when he was given the slates of success, he adapted them to the society he was living in at the time."

Norman finally was catching on that everyone who is entrusted with these principles will have to make changes to the society that they live in. He did not fear questioning me about the adaption made to the original principles, and he didn't make a statement, he just asked a poignant question. He finally learned that a question phrased in the right way can make a greater point then a direct statement.

"Norman, these changes were made because of the dire circumstances that North America has had to confront in the past twenty-five years."

He still had a confused look on his face.

"Do you believe that I have left something out?"

Norman spoke again. He didn't make a statement, as he had done earlier, wisely learned throughout our time together, instead he posed a question. "So, what do I do with all this information that you so generously bestowed onto me?" He continued with a follow-up. "Do I just apply these principles in life and profit from them as you have done?"

I responded, "Friend, meet me on Sunday morning, the fifth day of April, at 197 Granny Road in Farmingville. I will explain to you all the reasons why we met and what your future course of action will be in your life."

Sunday arrived, as if there were no Friday and Saturday between. I could see the look on Norman's face when he drove up to the driveway of the elementary school. Was he thinking that we were going to meet at a Ferrari dealership, Chase bank, or some other institution of great wealth? As he walked out of his sedan, you could tell that he was trying to conceive of the reason why I joined him at this children's school of fundamental learning.

I pulled the school keys out of my pocket, and he hesitantly followed me. After entering the vestibule, his eyes opened wide, and his head was on a swivel. He moved as if we were at the Museum of Natural History. We didn't speak; we just silently walked inside each class, observing the miniature sizes of the lockers, whiffing the smell of crayons in the air, spinning the reel of the pencil sharpeners, and smiling at the dimensions of the petite school chairs.

At the end of the self-tour, I walked directly to a display window that showed decades of photos, ribbons, certificates, and accolades. We both just stood there looking at some of the photos of the prior children who had attended that school. Then I looked over at Norman and asked him, "Do you think they were adequately instructed prior to being sent to their next phase of life?"

With a melancholic look on his dark face, he shrugged his head in the negative. Then he knew that wasn't my final question to him.

"Do you think that the students in junior high and high school are receiving adequate instructions to take on the challenges of the real world?"

He stood in a moment of silence, then I walked away from him. He followed me into a room where there was a podium. I took my position behind the pulpit and delivered the most eloquent speech that I have delivered since the case of The People v. John Gideon. It went as follows.

The Delivery of the Message

The numbness of society has reached a point that can no longer be ignored by its leaders, its parents, its clergy, and the common community. How is it that suicide is the second cause of death for our teenage children? Over three million teens from the ages of twelve to seventeen suffer from depression. In the United States alone over 40,000 people every year terminate their own lives. Why is suicide the number **one** *killer of men under the age of fifty? Accepting this is a tragedy! Yes, it is understood that this might not be your brother, your sibling, your spouse, or someone close to you, but you should realize it might come home one day!*

The opiate crisis! It is a tsunami that is leveling young adults throughout our country and sparing no one; no immunity is being granted from its death and destruction. It far surpasses the cocaine and crack epidemics of the 1980s and 1990s. The options are much more complex with opiates. I compare it to taking on and grappling with an octopus, there too many arms and tentacles . . . Adderall, Vicodin, opium, heroin, OxyContin, codeine, morphine, and methadone, just to mention a few.

In the past, the challenge was to prevent children from smoking marijuana, smoking cigarette, or drinking alcohol. Today they are being swarmed with endless opiate options. Norman, here we stand at this elementary school, which is like every other suburban elementary school in America, and, for that matter, urban and rural. I view it as if we are standing on hallowed ground, because it all begins here: humans' self-esteem, their self-worth, the way they see themselves, and how others see them. One's confidence is attained here, feeling accepted or rejected is nurtured or destroyed here, the ability to learn to speak intelligently with confidence begins here, and relationships with other little people are fostered or destroyed here.

We can't keep rejecting the notion that society

and particularly schools have no obligations to teach fundamental decision-making, team building, counseling and mentoring classes. The scientific community is in consensus that without these skills taught early in life, self-esteem, self-worth, bad decision-making, and depression become byproducts. This is not as difficult as it sounds and it can be taught concurrently with the main subjects. This is one of academia's highest callings. When you say to me, "Chemistry is a necessity," I say to you, "Coping methods, mentoring, and oratory methods are pound for pound more valuable!" Let's have this public debate!

Many people resort to negative options, because they believe that their lives are destined for failure. Somehow they have been convinced that others are greater, smarter, more gifted, and that others are more entitled to success. This is a head fake, in basketball terms. A head fake is not real but it is intended to make someone believe it is. It must be shown early in the lives of children that they too can become learned students; they too can deliver a worthy speech to an audience, and they too can master math and chemistry. Because, in reality, nothing is that difficult that can't be taught and learned by a motivated soul. Our belief system has been lost.

True believers exist. Here is the reality. In the US, there are over five million millionaires. There are over one million people in the US who make over $500,000 per year. According to the US Bureau of Labor Statistics, there are about 19 million people who own their own businesses. Over 60 percent of people in the US are homeowners. Approximately two million people have received law degrees; three million have received doctoral degrees, and over 40 percent of Americans have a college education. So the idea that you have to be the best in high school, college, or graduate school is a misnomer.

Owning your own business, your own home, or becoming a millionaire is not something that is out of the grasp of the average person. The real question is this: Do you wish to become that rare individual who surpasses life's expectations? How will you stand out as that special individual? America has been, and always will be, the land that anyone, including the one least expected, can become the most valuable. So, the desire to give up on your dreams earlier in life is a flaw in your personality that needs to be corrected.

There are wonderful things in this beautiful world that are rightfully yours. At what age should you no longer chase your dreams? My point is clear! Doesn't a ninety-year-old person still wish to see the majestic ocean, walk alongside the Grand Canyon, and hold hands with someone who loves them? It's a mistake to believe that you either get the gold medal or you fail in life. Extreme thinking is also a flaw in your character that needs to be corrected. Everything in between can still be successful. However, a majority of kids who do not reach their goals is because society, their parents, and their schools convinced them early in life that they are not worthy.

One of the notes Pierre left said the following.

> Comparing yourself to others is a fool's journey in that you can never become them and simultaneously you will lose the opportunity to find yourself.

"So, Norman, here is my injunction for you; here is why you were chosen to learn these methods and principles. This is the game plan, in essence the business plan that I propose to you. The numbers who are failing, giving up on life, and the numbers who are committing suicide are reaching levels that we have never witnessed in history. In the past, it was enough for some parents, some teachers, and some mentors to just encourage their children. This method of changing lives one person at a time, or one group at a time, is now futile.

"Drastic measures need to be taken to save millions from the endless traps that await them. If this trend does not get reversed, future generations of normal children will stand no chance to become highly successful in our society. Less than three decades ago, there were the rich, the middle class, and the poor. Because the principles of success have been lost and forgotten, a small portion of the middle class has shifted to the rich class and the vast majority are now labeled poor, bankrupt! In the next three decades, it will be the super-rich or the super-poor.

"Norman, you will be a pioneer in spreading these messages because of the system that you will utilize to attain maximum impact on the future generations. It will start at the elementary schools where you will teach, where you will lecture these principles near all the local schools. I will finance this project but your role is to teach the principles that you now have mastered.

"We can no longer sit around and not teach the future generations what the ancient generations understood. And, yes, I know that schools, including junior high schools and high schools will retain you to speak directly to their students. After the first group has graduated from the coursework of the slates of success, you will then choose a group of future mentors who will multiple the mission in each state. If my calculations are correct, we can be in or near every elementary school, junior high school, and high school in the next five years.

"But, as you have learned in all your lessons, it will not come easy, but it will happen. It's no different than planting our first seeds in a pot of soil and catering to it until the first stem arises, then the second, and so forth until you have a whole plant. There is a path of travel for all goals, and this will be no different, I assure you of that.

"Sorry, Norman, I must leave, you will find everything you need in the new box I left in your car. For some reason, I believe I have to leave you now, in my mind's eye I see Nadira seeking me."

Conclusion

Tomorrow has little value, yesterday has even less.
The future might appear, the past is forever gone.
                                    —Wilson A. LaFaurie, Esq.

After arriving at St. Charles Hospital, I asked the receptionist about the location of my wife. With the most compassionate voice I have ever heard, she instructed me about the route to her room, through the swinging metal doors, and follow the signs to the ICU. My walk toward those cold hallways to find Nadira's room was painful. Any distance between us felt like a twenty-six-mile marathon; distance was our enemy.

She knew my footsteps; she knew it was me walking down the long hallway. She expected me to find her in a haystack! With all the movement at the hospital and all the chattering, she was able to discern without the help of vision or eyesight that I was near. As I turned the corner, the last corner of the hospital corridor, her face was turned to the right of the entrance door to greet me.

In a whispering voice, she stated, "Your right foot hits the floor slightly harder than the left." She has never needed her senses of smell, touch, sound, or sight to know everything I think, feel, or do. I once told her that I think it was Adam who actually came from the rib of Eve, not the other way around.

I spent the next ten days in ICU with Nadira, some of the days I even slept in the hospital chair. Often when she would sleep, I would watch patients dying all alone. The nurse told me that it is common to see no spouse, no family, or no friends in some of those situations—seems ungodly. That was my only wish in life, to sleep in that room and not abandon her. It was a ghost town about 2:00 a.m., until the hospital equipment starting beeping for daily maintenance. That final night, she did not sleep. I did not sleep We just lay together on a one-person hospital bed with my head on her bosom. As I lay there, the biblical term of "Abraham's bosom" came to mind. At the same moment, the imagery of John the Apostle, leaning on Jesus' breast at the final supper becomes illuminating.

"Walter," she raised her head at me. "Sweet man, can you tell me something funny, something silly about when we lived in the house by the preserve?"

I would always abide by her wishes, as if she

were more my child than my spouse. She softly asked again with those deep, dark-brown eyes that were often mistaken for an onyx color. I took my hand and rubbed it through her thick hair. I just sat there and observed the beauty in her mixed culture of Indian and Guyanese. She repeated my name again, not having a hint of pushiness, but out of her liking to call on me.

"You remember all the details; you are so good at telling stories . . . I can see everything when you say it."

I always wondered why she loved for me to tell a story that she already knew the ending. "Ok, dollface! I remember one afternoon when I was working at home drafting a motion on a pro bono case for this poor family that was being evicted. I must have been on that computer for four hours without standing up."

She chimes in, surprises me with, "Where was Dante?" She knows that he is always thirsty and pees like a racehorse most of the time. My dog friend weighed 240 pounds at the time. When we purchased him, along with all the dog books, it was written that this Dogue de Bordeaux puppy would grow to a maximum weight of 175 pounds.

"I was so entrenched that I had forgotten about him. While I was typing, at some point I looked down, and he was looking straight at me. And you know, Dante. He was so lazy, he knew I would take him for a long walk. He would prefer to hold it for hours than to have to get up off the wooden floors. He just abhorred long walks.

"Because he despised the stairs, I picked him up (I still don't know why I loved to do that) and I carried him down the stairs. When I took him out the front door, Mrs. Cotton-Top, the old retired teacher, was in front of our lawn taking a walk. And she sees me struggling to carry Dante out the front of the house.

"As I squat down with him, being careful to bend my knees and not my back, Dante runs to the nearest tree and unleashes his fire hydrant, it was a projectile that bounced back onto him. It was endless, like two or three minutes of him assaulting the tree and the ricocheting of his pee back onto himself. As he was doing that, he turned and looked directly at me with this face of full contentment. He raised his right hind leg on the meat of the tree. Most dogs hold their own leg up in the air when they pee, not Dante, he places his leg on the tree. Why show should I be mad? He was like a human inside a dog!

"That day I didn't have time to take him in the woods for any exercise. Finally he was done releasing this hailstorm. Then, suddenly, I see the old woman, Mrs. Cotton-Top circling back near our house. I looked at Dante. He looked back at me and dropped to the ground, in the dirt with half his body coated with piss. Mrs. Cotton-Top decided to get a cramp in her calf, so she stopped and commenced to practice physical therapy on herself! Not a delightful image.

"So, in my most merciful way, I start calling Dante's name. "Come here, boy, Dante, time to come in . . . please?" As my desperation mounted, I kept begging for him to get up and come in. I pretend I have food in my hand. "I got beefy, Dante, Daddy got beefy!" He tilts his eyes slightly toward the location of my hand, as if he had infrared eyes, then lowered them once he was convinced that I was lying. I lose hope when he dropped his chin to the ground and just looked at me, then he looked back at Mrs. Cotton-Top, his eyes shifted back and forth, as if he were watching a Wimbledon match.

"As I come back into the house, Nadira has a cat-eating grin on her face and a bag of popcorn in one of her hands. She then proceeded to sit in her favorite chair and asked me to tell her the whole story of what just occurred outside. It took me about 20 minutes to articulate the Dante, Mrs. Cotton-Top story, because I knew she loved details and humor.

As I slow my storytelling, I see Nadira with a smile on her face, but with her eyes closed. I had not noticed until now that she had a letter in her hand. As I unfolded the letter, I realized it was something that I had written to her when we first met. I now share it with the world, since she is no longer with me.

July 31, 2008

The Poem for You

Happy anniversary. Happy birthday! Seven years
ago we met, stayed, and have celebrated ever since.
I wish to thank you for the last seven years. They
have been wonderful You have been wonderful.
Full of wonder, but wondering not.
You have smiled for seven years, I have always
wondered if your smile is the seventh wonder
of the world.
One would say that on that day we were made . . .
on your birthday.
Coincidence . . . not a chance. Happenstance . . .
not just a romance!
It is clear, to my ear that you are my dear . . .
right . . . Nadira?
Is it nature or nurture that makes our recipe?
Was it love at first sight or was it blind love?
Did they learn it from a book, or did they write
the book?
Ah, the passengers want to know the answer to the
greatest riddle!
How could he and she still be?
It is not to be written on this mere piece of scrap . . .
they must find it on the map.
But I am so cruel to leave you without a clue.

Pay attention here; it is clear; it is in your sight;
are you ready? . . .
Walter and Nadira walk in the sunlight and
became ONE.

Happy birthday, Nadira!

She would not have accepted me passing first.
She frequently spoke to me about this, as if I was the
decision-maker on the issue. I am grateful. I have joy
that her greatest torment did not become a reality . .
. being in this world without me.

Two years have passed since she left me. Often
she visits me in my dreams, where we have full
dinners, go out on dates, cook together, and we are
always talking about life. The dreams are always
different with full dialog and with our love affair
continuing, as if she never left.

One humid night, I fell asleep while reading *The
Count of Monte Cristo.* It was early, 8:17 p.m., and
I didn't wake until 6:00 a.m. As I awoke and lifted
my head, I noticed an object on Nadira's night table.
Was I seeing something? I cleared my eyes over and
over again. I noticed a piece of white fabric and her
favorite red pen on top of the small garment. I just
stared at this garment, because I knew that I did not

place it there, nor was it there on the previous night. Had I perhaps placed it there and forgotten.?

I cleared my eyes further and lean toward the fabric, and I now am able to see handwriting on the white fabric—one sentence with fifteen words. I elevate and draw the writing closer to my eyes. It was my handwriting! How could that be? Impossible that I wrote something. My hands started trembling, and I began crying like a child. I was whimpering and losing by breath, hyperventilating is the technical term for it.

The following was written in red ink.

> *The innermost feeling of failure is the innermost feeling of not knowing God.*

I never saw those words before. I have never used the word "innermost," and I was not cognizant of that sentence. Then I repeated the statement the other way around.

> *The innermost feeling of success is the innermost feeling of knowing God.*

In an instant, I was overcome with tranquility. I had never felt this sense of peace. I had been searching my whole life for tranquility, peace, and real truth, and finally those words were delivered to me. It is impossible for me to explain to you in a *natural sense* what happened to me in a *spiritual sense.* I will not try, but I do ask you to reread that sentence more than once. *That message was not delivered by human hands.* I am just the messenger.

I remember the grin that Pierre had when he said that, "Worldly success does not compare to spiritual success!" Pierre Smith, you old angelic man, I now understand and appreciate why you paid me that visit so long ago.

Acknowledgments

This book could not have been created, if not for my birth parents, Antonio LaFaurie and Teresa LaFaurie.

The professionalism and expertise in editing and designing this book by Deborah Perdue of Illumination Graphics and her team far surpassed my expectations. One would think that it was their book the way they treated its development.

I will always be grateful to UDC David A. Clarke School of Law for giving this imperfect student an opportunity to prove he could compete with the Ivy Leaguers.

To my wife, Sharon, for telling me for years that I should write this book—your excitement encouraged me throughout this difficult but worthy journey!

Connect with Me

Website: SlatesofSuccess.com
Email: Lafaurie@optonline.net
Facebook: Wilson LaFaurie
Twitter: Wilson A. LaFaurie@lafaurielaw

CPSIA information can be obtained
at www.ICGtesting.com
Printed in the USA
BVHW04s0955051018
529241BV00021BA/759/P